One Day in April

One Day in April

Hillsborough: A Mother's Story

Jenni Hicks

SEVEN DIALS

First published in Great Britain in 2022 by Seven Dials
this paperback edition published in 2023 by Seven Dials,
an imprint of The Orion Publishing Group Ltd
Carmelite House, 50 Victoria Embankment
London EC4Y 0DZ

An Hachette UK Company

1 3 5 7 9 10 8 6 4 2

ISBN (Mass Market Paperback) 9781409196242
ISBN (eBook) 9781409196259
ISBN (Audio) 9781409196266

Typeset by Born Group
Printed and bound in Great Britain by Clays Ltd, Elcograf S.p.A.

MIX
Paper from
responsible sources
FSC
www.fsc.org   FSC® C104740

www.orionbooks.co.uk

This book has been written by me in everlasting memory of my beautiful daughters, Sarah Louise and Victoria Jane Hicks.
You are my shining lights on the path to truth and justice.

'Injustice anywhere is a threat to justice everywhere.'
Martin Luther King, Jr

Dear Reader

On the morning of 15 April 1989 my husband Trevor and I, and our daughters Sarah and Vicki, set off to watch Liverpool FC play in an FA Cup semi-final at the Hillsborough football stadium in Sheffield.

That night Trevor and I drove back alone. Our two daughters were left in body bags on a dirty gymnasium floor at the football ground.

Within hours we, an ordinary family, were headline news. What followed were years of lies, cover-up and deceit, loss, grief, break-up and divorce.

This is the story of how I have attempted to cope with it all.

Jenni Hicks, March 2022

Chapter 1

It was a lovely spring day in April when the flowers finally came into bloom: a mass of red and yellow tulips that matched the latest Liverpool Football Club strip. We lived in London, but my daughters, Sarah, nineteen, and Vicki, fifteen, were avid Liverpool supporters. That previous autumn they had planted dozens of bulbs alternately, one red, one yellow and so on, all the way round the borders of the lawn and down the steps to the house, which now looked amazing. It was coming towards the end of the Easter holidays, when Vicki was due back at school and my husband Trevor would be driving Sarah back to Liverpool to begin her third term at university before going on to his flat in Dudley to start the working week in nearby Kingswinford. But there was one big event the girls were really looking forward to before then, just as I was. On the last Saturday of the holidays, 15 April 1989, Liverpool were playing Nottingham Forest in the semi-final of the FA Cup at Hillsborough football stadium, Sheffield. The Reds were riding a wave, and Trevor, the girls and I all had tickets for the game and were going to travel up to Sheffield to watch Liverpool win.

Sarah was tall, elegant and beautiful with big blue eyes, blond hair and striking features, and my friend Chris would often say she resembled Princess Di. Sarah had style and class and looked good in whatever she chose to wear. Kind and generous and always helpful to others, she didn't have a competitive bone in her body (except when it came to watching Liverpool FC play!) and was as beautiful on the inside as she was outside. She was also intellectually very bright and was given the opportunity to go to Oxford, and was offered a scholarship at Imperial College London to read Chemistry, but she'd had other ideas. Towards the end of the Easter holidays Sarah had asked me to help lighten her hair where her dark roots were coming through. Then she'd permed mine into an eighties wiggly style in preparation for my return to work in the earth sciences department of our local sixth-form college on the Monday after the match.

Vicki, who was three years younger than her big sister, was a few inches shorter and had the biggest cornflower blue eyes you'd ever seen. She also had beautiful long dark hair and a fashion style very different to Sarah's. Vicki could melt anyone's heart with just a look. She was funny without even realising it – she could always manage to make people smile. When she was little, strangers in the street would come up to her and pat her on the head and comment on how cute she was. Vicki liked to put on a strong exterior, she was ambitious and liked nice things, but inside she was a sensitive soul with a heart of gold. And, like Sarah, she couldn't bear social injustice.

During the Easter holiday, I would hear Vicki playing her music upstairs. If Sarah was in her room at the time, she would put her music on too. The next thing I knew, Vicki would turn hers up, and then Sarah, until U2 and Frankie Goes to Hollywood were blaring out from their rooms on the landing as the girls tried to outdo each other.

'I'm trying to study here, tell her, Mum!' Vicki, in her A-ha T-shirt and baggy jeans, yelled down the stairs. She had been working hard most days over the Easter period in preparation for her GCSEs that she was taking at her school in Elstree, but this wasn't one of those days! She'd spent all afternoon going through her reel-to-reel tapes from the charts and playing them back while setting out all her earrings in neat rows on the dressing table.

'Turn that music down, the pair of you!' I yelled up the stairs.

It was just as well we lived in a large detached house where we couldn't bother the neighbours, as there was a lot of door-slamming between the music and the shouting. But I knew it would be all right later because, for all their arguments and getting on each other's nerves, the girls were fiercely loyal and always, always had each other's back. And that would be the case until their very last breath.

The day before the much-anticipated semi-final at Hillsborough, Sarah had spent the morning packing in preparation for going back to uni the day after the match. It was a gorgeous, warm, sunny day for the time of year, and so in the afternoon Sarah and Vicki opted to sunbathe in the back garden – they wanted a tan. The three of us were having such a lovely, relaxing day that although I was supposed to be doing the weekly shop, I decided not to bother. In any case, I was due back at work at Stanmore sixth-form college the following week, so I thought I would just enjoy the day too.

As we sat out in the sun, Vicki suddenly announced that

her eyebrows needed plucking. Typical Vicki! She wanted her eyebrows to look good for the semi-final, so I drove her to a beautician's in Hatch End.

Strangely, although Trevor would usually arrive home late every Friday night, on this occasion he came home early. Vicki and I had just got back from the beauticians when she said, 'I really fancy a Cornetto.' So, she and Trevor went to Waitrose to get the ice creams and a few bits of shopping for dinner as well. When they got back, Vicki produced a box of mint Cornettos from the shopping bag, and I said to her, 'Let's have the proper food first and then you can have the Cornetto.'

But after the meal no one was hungry, so we said we would have the ice creams on Saturday night when we got back from the Hillsborough match. I made a picnic lunch for us for the next day, as usual, and we all went to bed. I didn't realise that this would turn out to be our final day together.

The following morning, we got up early to set off for our family day out. There was a lot of excitement because it was the semi-final, but Vicki typically couldn't decide which T-shirt to wear with her jeans.

I called up the stairs a couple of times, 'Vicki, we're ready to go!' Sarah and I were waiting downstairs, and Trevor was in the car getting more and more impatient.

She finally emerged in a white T-shirt with a large motif on the front, long navy grandad cardigan, baggy jeans and brown boots tied with green laces. Then, putting in her favourite earrings, she shrugged, 'What's all the fuss about?' and we set off for the game.

Chapter 2

I am proud to say that Liverpool is now my adopted home and where I have lived for over thirty years. It is where my heart is and the place where I can still be close to my girls, but I was actually born in County Durham and brought up a few miles away, over the border in Yarm, North Yorkshire. Although I had a very happy childhood, as an adult I came to realise that my early life was not like other people's and, to this day, it's still something of a mystery to me. However, I believe my childhood and the differences that set me apart helped me to develop the resilience and strength I would need many years later to survive the loss of my children and to fight for justice for them, a struggle that would go on for over thirty years.

I was just six months old when my mum, Rose Peat, took me to a bus stop in Stockton-on-Tees and gave me away. Of course, I was only a baby so I have no memory of what happened that day, but I'm told she handed me over to Mrs Broadley, the policeman's wife, who was standing in the queue. She lived next door to my paternal grandmother in Yarm, four and a half miles away. My mum and dad continued living in Stockton and having more children. But for the next eleven years of my life I would be brought up by my grandparents, Helen and Jack Peat, who were already in their seventies at that point. My dad's siblings – Tommy, Stan, Lizzie, and her teenage son, Lawrence, or Lol as we called him – also lived there. And with Dad's other brother, Uncle Alfie, living across the road with his wife and twin sons, I had family all around me.

My new home with Granny Peat was a three-bedroom, 1940s-built council house in Coronation Crescent, Yarm: a semi-rural location with fields at the back. With seven of us living there, it was always a busy house, and whenever Granny had visitors they would be ushered into the front room. Granny brought chair backs for the sofa and armchairs to stop Lol and my uncles getting grease on them from the Brylcreem they used to slick back their short-back-and-sides. When I stop and reflect, I can still hear the ticking of the clock on the mantelpiece, and see the grinning Toby jugs either side of it. Above the fireplace was a mirror where Auntie Lizzie, with her large hazel eyes and thick auburn hair, would slap on her Pond's face cream. Auntie was naturally pretty and didn't wear make-up. The front-room walls were covered with photographs of relatives long gone before I'd arrived. Beside the dining table was a china cabinet where the best tea service was kept, and only brought out for Christmas, weddings and funerals, and other special occasions. Granny wasn't house-proud but, if it had been raining, she'd insist my uncles and cousin who lived with us took off their work boots each evening and left them by the back door; that's as far as it went though.

Despite not having much, it was a comfortable home. At the time, we were the only family in our street to boast a television set. I'm not sure how Granny afforded it, but it was her pride and joy. As a child, she'd tell me how she'd invited the entire street round to watch the Queen's Coronation. Auntie Lizzie, who had previously been in service to a family in an affluent area of Manchester, helped Gran with the household chores every week. On Wednesdays she'd put down some old newspaper, then polish the stairs rods with Brasso until you could see your face in them, while Grandma shone the horse brasses around the fireplace.

At mealtimes we would all get together as a family, sitting around the big table in the 'back-kitchen' as it was called, while Granny got our dinner ready. Her staples were things like steak-and-kidney pudding and stew and dumplings. Amazing smells always came from the kitchen, Gran was such a great cook. But fridge-freezers were not available to ordinary folk then, so she had to store everything in the walk-in pantry. This included the rabbits my uncle Alfie, a gamekeeper, would bring us and which Granny would keep on a shelf until she was ready to make a pie or stew with them. Seeing those poor lifeless creatures lying there would make me feel sad, but I still enjoyed the dishes Grandma made with them.

Uncle Stan was the youngest of Dad's brothers and Gran's favourite of her four sons, which meant that any second helpings that were going, he'd always get them. Though, being the baby of the family, I didn't do so badly myself. My cousin Lol was the next one to me in age but he was in his late teens when I arrived there. I remember getting into bed one night and letting out a scream when something prickly touched my leg – only to see Lol doubled up with laughter on the landing. 'Gotcha!' he said, as I found the scrubbing brush that he'd hidden in there. Lol, who was good-looking, well dressed and very popular with the girls, was always joking around.

Grandad and my uncles all wore cloth caps and, looking back now, I realise we were a true working-class family – we worked to live. Indeed, the biggest fear in our house was not having a job so, to earn a bit extra, my uncles would work for the local farmers on their days off, particularly during harvest time. We had a big garden where we grew our own vegetables, and an allotment where my uncles kept pigs, ducks, geese and hens for eggs. There were apple trees and pear trees too. My uncles and I would go out mushrooming, and in the early autumn we'd pick blackberries from the hedgerows to make jam and puddings with. It was a country childhood and we saved a lot of money by being self-sufficient.

Our biggest, most prized, mod con was an inside bathroom and a toilet. Few houses boasted such a luxury at the time, but we only had a coal fireplace in the front room. On winter nights it would get so cold, icicles would form *inside* the windows. So Granny made sure no one went to bed without two hot-water bottles each. How I loved the comforting smell of those rubbery hot-water bottles, one of which I would hug to me while the other went on my feet.

The coal was delivered each week by the coalman, 'Watch those sacks now, our Jennifer!' Granny would call to me as I stood on the back step and counted the sacks emptied into the coalhouse. Granny had no intention of paying for more than the coalman delivered. Looking back, I learned a lot

8

from my granny, but one of the lessons that's stuck with me most is that you always have to watch out for yourself and, if anyone tries to take advantage of you, you must be prepared to fight your corner.

We may have been poor, but I had a charmed existence growing up with my extended family in North Yorkshire. Yarm is a beautiful tree-lined little town with a cobbled high street and Georgian houses either side. Perhaps the horse-shoe-shaped River Tees running around the town brought me luck, as I loved my life there. The bridge which crosses the river still forms the border between North Yorkshire and County Durham, which Mrs Broadley and I would have crossed on the bus on the day when Mum, who was pregnant with my brother by then, sent me to Granny.

Everyone knew everyone else and I felt safe there. My Uncle Alfie's twin sons were only a few months younger than me so I had two ready-made playmates in the street. I used to love being in my cousins' cricket team, playing out in the summer and using an old orange box for a wicket. My daughter Sarah would take after me: she loved games too and was a tomboy just like me when she was younger.

As I grew up, I became close to Mrs Broadley, who was as wide as her name suggests, and her policeman husband, Bert, who was rarely out of uniform. As a child, he was how I saw policemen, and I realised what an important job he had. He was somebody everyone respected. The Broadleys would always make a big fuss of me. 'Come round any time, Jennifer!' Mrs Broadley would say, and she'd make a chocolate cake especially for me. Their house was posh inside compared to ours. They had a sofa with plump cushions on it and a fitted carpet that went right up to the edges of the walls, not cold lino everywhere like us. There were shelves all the way along one of the walls, full of wonderful books and encyclopaedias, which I'd take out and gaze at for hours. We really only had local newspapers in our house for the sport; books like the Broadleys had would become so important to me later on, particularly legal ones, when I began looking for justice for my girls.

Although ours was a matriarchal family with Granny in charge, Grandad would keep my uncles and Lol in line. Even when they were strapping men, Grandad didn't have to say a word: one look from him was enough. They never answered him back or swore in front of him or Granny, the way they did when they were out.

My grandparents, like most parents in the neighbourhood, sent all their children to Sunday school. I started when I was six years old. On Sunday lunchtimes at twelve o'clock Uncle Tommy and Uncle Stan would go to the local pub and stay there until at two o'clock, when Granny and Auntie Lizzie would have the Sunday roast dinner on the table. After dinner they always fell asleep in the two big armchairs in the living room. Then at three o'clock, dressed in my best clothes, I would go to Sunday school at the Wesleyan chapel with the other local children.

Unlike some of the children who attended, I relished going each week and loved hearing the stories about Jesus and parables, like the Good Samaritan. The message I learned there was this: if you were good, Jesus wouldn't let anything bad happen to you. I found that very comforting as a six-year-old. I also liked ringing the little bells on the wooden rack. Problem was, you were only allowed to ring them when it was your birthday, whereas I would go up to ring them regularly – until the teacher noticed and I was told off.

Although there are huge parts of my early life that I don't remember, I do remember ringing those bells. It was the kind of cheeky thing my Vicki would get up to when she was little.

As soon as Sunday school ended, it would be time to go home for tea and to see my dad, who came to visit me at Granny's every Sunday. Granny always laid on a big tea then, when all the family were expected to attend in their best clothes. My dad would put on his suit, even though he looked stiff and uncomfortable in it. Granny would make tinned-salmon sandwiches, followed by what I'd now call a 'deconstructed trifle', which was a bowl of jelly, another of custard, one of tinned fruit and another of cream that Granny did especially for my dad, who liked all those things separately but insisted he didn't like trifle!

Every Sunday, Dad would bring one of my younger siblings with him to visit. My brother John was born a year after me, and Mum and Dad then had another two sons, Barrie and the baby of the family, David, so they'd all get a turn coming to their Granny Peat's every three weeks. But I never expected my mum to come over, as I knew by now that she wouldn't. She never came to Yarm, and my granny never went to my parents' house. No one in our house ever spoke badly about Mum, they all liked her, so I have no idea why she never came, but I would still see my parents regularly, and remain close to my dad, Chris. In my mind, I was just a normal, happy kid with what was, to me, a normal childhood, growing up in a house full of kind, caring people. I knew I was loved by my grandparents and I never doubted I was loved by my parents too, even though my mum was more like an auntie to me.

When I was nine or ten, I went most evenings to ballet and tap at Connie Hall's School of Dancing in Stockton. Every Wednesday evening Aunt Lizzie would take me to visit my mum and dad's afterwards. Their house was a dark, two-up two-down in a street of identical crumbling Victorian terraces. Even at the tender age I was then, it wasn't difficult to see my parents were struggling and poorer even than us. They didn't even have a bathroom; my dad and brothers had to get washed at the kitchen sink and on a Friday night my mum would bring in the tin bath that was kept outside on a peg in the yard. Mum had to heat up water in the copper boiler to fill it, and then the family would take turns to use it. It was a Friday-night ritual at their house, which made me glad we had a proper bath at home with hot water coming out of the taps, and a house surrounded by countryside.

There was always a strange musty smell about my parents' house too, which would make me feel nauseous. I later realised it was the smell of damp – all the houses in the road were condemned, with families on the council list waiting to be rehoused, so Mum always kept a big roaring open fire going in the living room to try to keep the damp at bay. But if we went on Saturday afternoons, there was a real weekend treat: my mum would go to the Sparks Bakery and buy a box of six cream cakes for the whole family. And I would get the pick of the cakes, because everyone else would have theirs for Sunday tea. There was always a good selection – strawberry tarts, chocolate eclairs, meringues filled with cream – it was like looking into a jewellery box. Granny always frowned on 'bought cakes'; she insisted everything had to be homemade.

Although I was always pleased to see my parents, it never occurred to me to ask to stay and, by the end of the evening, I was ready to go back to my granny and to the home I was used to. My dad would walk me and Auntie Lizzie to the same bus stop where my mum had handed me over all those years ago, but I wasn't aware of that then; instead, I was more interested in the fish-and-chip shop alongside it. 'Ooh, they smell nice!' I used to say, and Dad would disappear into the shop, returning with a bag of chips for me to eat on the bus on the way home.

When I think back, I have nothing but pride and admiration for my dad, who worked his fingers to the bone to make enough money to feed his growing family, and admiration for my mum too, who brought up three strong boys in what were undeniably tough conditions. When I became a parent myself, I wanted my girls to have many of the things that my family and I didn't have, but I also wanted to bring them up to be independent, fair-minded and resilient to whatever life threw at them when they went out into the world, as I'd learned to be. But most of all, kind and loved. I know I succeeded.

Looking back, football was one of the defining experiences of my childhood. When I'd come home from seeing my mum on a Wednesday evening, the midweek match would be on the radio and my uncles would be poring over the sports section of the papers, working out the score draws to put on their football coupons that might win them a fortune at the weekend. Then on Saturdays it was football crazy at our house, with the TV on and heated discussions about the teams and how our local team Middlesbrough or Boro were doing. At quarter to five, my uncles would all huddle round the radio in the back-kitchen waiting for James Alexander Gordon to read out the scores while they checked the results against their coupon copies. 'We're going to make our fortunes today!' Uncle Tommy would say to me as he rubbed his hands in anticipation – only to chuck the coupon away in disgust after the results came in. Everyone would be moaning then: if only they'd put this score and not that and gone with their instinct, or some such. It was a family ritual!

On occasion, my uncles would take me to Boro's home matches at Ayresome Park. They'd take me as a special treat, as, with a child in tow, they couldn't go to a pub afterwards for the usual match post-mortem. I was small even as a child and when we arrived at the game, they'd shout, 'Watch out, child coming over!' then hand me over the heads of the other Boro supporters and sit me on the high barriers, where I could get a bird's-eye view of the game.

I especially loved the Wednesday-night games when my uncles and I would travel to the ground on the 'football specials', which were double-decker buses laid on to take supporters to a match. With all the camaraderie and banter between the fans on those double-decker buses, it built up the excitement before the game. When we'd get there, I loved seeing the pitch and the players all lit up by the floodlights, and even though Boro were struggling near the bottom of Division Two and often lost at the time, that didn't matter to me as the atmosphere was electric when the team came on. Although I was small, I remember so clearly when Boro's new signing, a young player called Brian Clough, made his first appearance in the club's shirt on the home ground. The fans began to go wild as he knocked in goal after goal in his first few games alone, and he steadily and single-handedly improved the club's position over the next few years. Though Boro never went up to the First Division, Clough was a brilliant player and, while he naturally moved on after he made his name at Boro, he made a lasting impression. How different these feelings toward him were in comparison to the next time I would see him when he was manager of Nottingham Forest and we were on opposing sides in the fateful FA Cup semi-final at Hillsborough. The comments he would make about the Liverpool fans after that semi-final carried weight because he'd been there that day. Seeing footage of him now, and hearing his opinions, sadly, makes me feel sick to the pit of my stomach.

Chapter 3

I loved going to our local school. I enjoyed every minute of it and made lots of friends there. Because I was so tiny for my age, our infant teacher, Miss Mackie, would make me climb a stepladder in my net tutu and wings to be the fairy on top of the tree in the Christmas show! It made Granny and Auntie laugh when they came to see me. It's strange to think that my lack of height, along with my girls' insistence that I take the seated ticket for the game, would years later play a vital role in my surviving the Hillsborough disaster.

I passed my eleven-plus and was offered a place at the local grammar school. But my granny and uncles thought it would be too expensive and wasted on a girl whose only 'job' was to get married and have babies. My family weren't being unkind; working-class children were expected to go out to work as soon as they could, to contribute to the family income. I wasn't disappointed. I was pleased to be staying on in the senior part of the local school that I was already attending.

I was nine years old when I first experienced loss. Auntie Lizzie had taken me to a dancing competition in South Shields in the Easter holidays where dance schools from all over the north-east came to compete. First prize was a gold medal and a silver cup. We left home early that Saturday morning to make sure I got there on time. Auntie was really proud of my success, and on the way back she made sure everyone on the coach home got sight of the gold medal and silver cup I'd won! It was such a happy journey back, and I was bursting to tell Granny I'd won and show her the silver cup.

But as soon as we got off the coach in our road, we saw all the curtains were drawn at our house, even though it was still daylight. In those days, closed curtains meant only one thing – someone had died. Granny was crying when we went into the house and my uncles were upset; Grandad had suddenly passed away. I couldn't mention my success or show Granny my trophies because it wasn't the time for it, and it never would be. Granny went into mourning and from that day onwards there was something about her that was lost, never to return. Less than two years later, she passed away too. We were all devastated. Granny had been the centre of our home, and she had been both my grandmother and my mum. Despite how I felt, I didn't cry; I felt numb. I had been brought up to get on with whatever life threw at you, and that's what I tried to do.

Granny was buried with my grandad at Yarm cemetery. As her coffin was lowered into the ground, my twin cousins and I each threw a red rose onto it. It was the first time I'd been to a funeral and I found it bleak and frightening; none of the ceremony reminded me about the fun, laughter and colourful times we'd had with Granny. It felt wrong, somehow. Afterwards, we went back to the house for a do put on by the Co-op funeral service. Granny had always been into good send-offs and she reckoned the Co-op did the best ones. Her friends and neighbours all came to the tea.

The next day I was back in school, my uncles went back to work and Auntie Lizzie carried on cleaning the brasses, but sadness had settled over the house. Even so, every Sunday after Granny passed, Auntie Lizzie would put the roast on as Granny had, and then she and I would walk to the cemetery to put fresh flowers on my grandparents' graves – just as I would do years later for my own girls, Sarah and Vicki.

One of the things that became a huge help and healer for me after Grandma passed was a little golden Labrador puppy that Uncle Tommy came home with one day to try to cheer us all up. She was a pedigree registered with the Kennel Club, and he'd done a deal in the pub with a local farmer. They gave her some fancy Kennel Club name like Salome Fascination, but you couldn't shout that out in the fields where we walked her, so we settled for Judy instead.

Judy had recently left her mum when she came to live with us and was so nervous, the poor little thing would shake all the time. So to make her feel more at home we made her a cosy bed at the bottom of a warm cupboard in the back-kitchen. But Judy still cried so we tried her with a soft toy and a hot-water bottle, but that didn't work either. Auntie Lizzie and Uncle Tommy told me to stop worrying, that she'd soon settle in, but I felt so sorry for her that I would creep down in the middle of the night, scoop her up and take her back up to bed with me, where we'd cuddle up together and quickly drop off to sleep. I think we were a comfort to each other, and it was worth all the telling offs I got from Auntie and Uncle when they discovered she'd been in my bed again!

★

By my early teens my best friend Ann from school and I got into pop music and fashion. On Friday evenings and weekends when there were no dance classes, I'd meet up with Ann and we'd play music at each other's houses or hang out at the local coffee bar and chat with some of the boys from the Boys' Brigade. I guess I did cause Auntie some concerns, but gradually laughter began to return to the house once again.

Although my dad and uncles were still Boro supporters, by this time I was into Spurs and Manchester United, not least because, as regards the latter team, I had a thing about the gorgeous and talented George Best. One weekend my friend Janet and her boyfriend Bernard came to stay at my house in Yarm. Bernard was from Liverpool, and when he found out I was a Manchester United supporter, he nearly choked!

He gave me a look as if I was crazy. 'You want to start supporting a decent team,' he said in his Scouse accent. Although the conversation was just light-hearted banter, it is true to say that no matter how badly Boro performed (and by then we'd been relegated to the Third Division) my uncles were never fair-weather supporters and still went to their games. However, after speaking to Bernard, for some reason I started looking out for Liverpool too. I suppose I was intrigued to see why he thought they were so great. But I think also it was because Liverpool had produced the biggest band on earth, the Beatles, whose music and films I'd grown up on and adored. Even though the Beatles had left Liverpool by this time, it still boasted the Mersey Sound, the Cavern Club, the Liverpool Poets, and *The Liver Birds* sitcom was set there. It was a 'happening' place that, for a short while, was rivalling the London scene. Unfortunately for me, I couldn't go to Liverpool, let alone see any of LFC's games. We lived too far away, and we couldn't afford a car. So instead, I would watch Liverpool FC play on *Match of the Day* and later on ITV's *The Big Match*.

It was at this time when the club was really taking off. The legendary Bill Shankly had brought them into the First Division and the following season, 1963–64, they won the League, followed by the FA Cup the season after when they played Leeds at Wembley, with Ian St John scoring the winner. Roger Hunt, who was top scorer for Liverpool eight seasons in a row, was another great player at the club. As soon as he ran out onto the pitch, the fans would burst into a round of 'Wonderful Roger' to the tune of the Wonderloaf advert that was on ITV at the time. Roger so delighted the fans that they dubbed him 'Sir Roger', although possibly the nearest he ever got to royalty and being knighted was playing Palace at Selhurst Park.

It was the FA Cup of 1965, when Liverpool beat Leeds 2-1, that I really started to take notice. This would begin my lifelong love for Liverpool: the city, the football team and its people.

Chapter 4

When I left school at fifteen, I began a two-year course at the local tech college where I passed several O levels. I was thankful to have had a decent head at my old school who'd suggested the college course, because those qualifications set me in good stead: helping me to get a clerical job in Stockton when I left, and later on when I was looking for a mortgage.

I'd thrown in my dancing by this time and Auntie Lizzie, who was bitterly disappointed by this, having enjoyed watching me win my many medals, suddenly became aware of a craze that was sweeping the nation: bingo. As dozens of local cinemas closed down every week, so new bingo halls opened in their place. How well I remember Auntie pulling on the box jacket that went with her pencil skirt, saying, 'Well, I'll give it a go this Saturday, but don't hold your breath.' She ended up going four nights a week every week for years, and she loved it!

There would be a dance for teenagers in Yarm Village Hall every Saturday night, with a rock 'n' roll band playing, and I would go with my friends and meet boys there, including the local heart-throb, Derek. He looked so cool with his blond hair in a quiff like Billy Fury, but with so many girls after him I didn't think I stood a chance. So, when he asked me out on a date I thought all my Christmases had come at once, and by the following year we were engaged. If Sarah or Vicki had turned up years later, engaged at seventeen to a Billy Fury lookalike, I would have been devasted! But Auntie Lizzie, Uncle Tommy and Derek's parents were all delighted. It wasn't long though before Derek bumped into an ex-girlfriend and dumped me for her. I was heartbroken and there was nothing anyone could do or say to make me feel any better.

After a few weeks of staying home feeling sorry for myself, my friend Linda from the travel agency where I worked persuaded me to go to a dance with her at the Astoria in Middlesbrough. My life would change forever when she introduced me to her ex-boyfriend that very first night. His name was Trevor. He was dark-haired, good-looking, and I fancied him straight away. The feeling must have been mutual, as the next day Trevor turned up on his motorbike at Linda's home. Linda's mum called to Linda, thinking he was there to take her out, but then he told her he'd come to see me! Once we began going out together, he'd turn up every evening on his motorbike when he wasn't studying at night school. Trevor lived ten miles from me and was serving a mechanical engineering apprenticeship with ICI which, when he finished it, was expected to lead to a secure job. Although Uncle Tommy always enjoyed a chat with Trevor whenever he came around, Auntie Lizzie did not take to him at all – and she didn't try to hide it. Fortunately, she was still going to bingo most nights. By this time Uncle Stan and Lol had both got married and moved into their own homes, so whenever Uncle Tommy was at work and Auntie Lizzie was at bingo, Trevor and I had the house to ourselves. On Auntie's return she would say, 'You've got work in the morning, our Jennifer,' accompanied by loud yawning to encourage Trevor to leave. She would never go to bed and leave us alone downstairs. Little did Auntie know that the very thing she worried about us getting up to had already happened while she was at the bingo hall waiting for 'Eyes Down' to be called.

Six months after we met, Trevor and I got engaged. We paid £25 each for an old Hillman Minx, which was maroon and cream with cream leather upholstery inside. Instead of two separate front seats it had one long front bench, which was great for cuddling up on when it was cold, and other things too. Nobody in my family had ever owned a car before and I felt really lucky.

The following June, six months after the engagement, we got married at St Mary Magdalene's church, Yarm. I wore a long, empire line dress made for me by Mrs Etheridge, the lady who ran up the dresses for our dancing shows. It was so beautiful that when I went for the final fitting, I was really worried I wouldn't be able to afford it. However, Mrs Etheridge wasn't having any of it.

'You are not paying a penny, it is my wedding gift to you,' she said.

I was so touched by her kindness, and relieved too, as we had so little money. By this time I had become used to adapting to my circumstances and being pragmatic, and with Trevor's help we made the best of it. In fact, Trevor had managed to mould some fine wire into a tiara for me at his dad's garage, and then set it with diamonds from an old necklace he'd taken apart. It looked fab, and set off my auburn hair beautifully.

Having had an unusual childhood, rather than follow the usual marriage traditions, I wanted Uncle Tommy to give me away. This caused an almighty row.

'That's not right,' Uncle Alfie protested, 'it should be your dad.'

But because I'd grown up with Uncle Tommy, he felt more like a dad to me, and instinctively I thought he should be the one.

We couldn't afford a honeymoon, so after a reception with a buffet at the Black Bull in Yarm, Trevor carried me over the threshold of our new home. This was a little flat we were renting in Stockton, while we tried to save every penny we could to scrape together enough for a deposit to buy our own home one day. With Trevor still earning peanuts as an apprentice and me able to earn more than him from the travel agent job, within a year we'd managed to make a deposit on our very first home. This was a new-build Wimpy home at Thornaby near Stockton, south of the River Tees. It was nothing special by today's standards, but to me it was everything, and it symbolised how much I could achieve if I worked hard and put my mind to it. A lesson that stayed with me when I raised my girls, and later on when I faced my biggest challenge in life.

My family were so proud to see I had got my own house too. People like us had only ever been able to afford to rent and here were Trevor and I, at twenty-one, with our own place! I only wished Granny and Grandad could have seen it; I know they'd have been pleased for me. I think my mum would have been made up too. Over the last few years, Mum and I had finally started to become closer, until tragedy struck and once again someone I loved was taken away. Mum was only fifty-four. Although she'd never really played a major role in my life and had only ever come to see me perform once in all the years that I'd danced, when she did turn up, she was so proud of me and she loved to show me off. It was a loss, but I didn't realise what an important loss until much later, when I had children of my own.

As I got older and began to understand more, I would've loved to have had a conversation with my mum, woman to woman, about why she sent me to live at my granny's, and why she never visited. I would also have loved her to see what I would make of my life and particularly to meet her two beautiful granddaughters Sarah and Vicki when they came along, but that wasn't to be.

I was mourning for what might have been rather than what I'd lost, and for what my mum had lost. I'd never got to know any of her side of the family either, though I knew she had several brothers and sisters. At the funeral tea, the only person I recognised from the maternal side was my mum's mother, who announced halfway through that she had to dash to play a game of darts at the pub! She was a member of a local darts team and they had a match that evening. She was in her early nineties by this time, and partial to rum. One way or another, I guess you could say I had two very strong grandmothers. Perhaps I've inherited something of their characters.

ONE DAY IN APRIL

Chapter 5

Not long after moving to Thornaby, I fell pregnant with Sarah. Trevor and I were both so excited and happy with this news. However, when the nausea I had suffered in the first couple of weeks turned into full-blown all-day nausea and vomiting, it was awful. The only foods my body didn't reject were fresh peaches and fish and chips, of all things! These became my staple diet – I would literally crave them night and day, sometimes sending Trevor out at night to fetch some.

It became a struggle to carry on with my job, but as attitudes to pregnant women in the workplace were very different then I knew once I got to six months I would be asked to leave. Leaving work at six months suited me fine, and enabled me the luxury of spending twelve weeks at home to prepare for Sarah's arrival.

Three years later, I was pregnant with Vicki and this time it would be scrambled eggs, bacon and Cadbury's choco-late mini rolls that I craved. Even now, every time I see a chocolate mini roll or eat a peach, I think of those times.

After a long and difficult labour with my first pregnancy, I was given an emergency C-section and little Sarah Louise arrived on 10 April 1970. Because Sarah had nearly died during labour, she was immediately taken to the intensive care baby unit, so I didn't get to hold her for the first forty-eight hours, until she was out of danger. As soon as I recovered from the general anaesthetic, a nurse took me in a wheelchair to see her, where I viewed her for the first time through a glass screen. She was tiny with gorgeous thick dark hair and she looked absolutely beautiful. I know every mother says that, but it really was true. She was stunning.

When they finally said I could hold Sarah, she looked so fragile I was too frightened to take her from the midwife. The midwife tried to reassure me, 'You'll make all your mistakes with the first one, and you'll know what you're doing by the time you have the second.' These were wise words.

Placing this little bundle in my arms, it began to sink in that, yes, I was a mum! And I was overjoyed! As I looked at her while she slept, her beautiful face and long eyelashes, it made me realise she was the most precious gift I could ever receive, and there wasn't anything I wouldn't do to protect her.

Being a new mum, I was lucky that Sarah was a particularly easy baby. She had no problems feeding, she soon slept through the night and by the time she was a year old she was walking and talking. Looking back, it felt in some ways that Sarah never really was a baby.

When Auntie Lizzie came to visit she noticed something special about Sarah too, and said, 'That baby's been here before.' I didn't know what she meant.

'Sarah, she's so advanced,' she explained, 'I think she's been here before.'

And it was true. She was advanced in talking, walking and feeding herself, but because she was my first child, I had nothing to compare her milestone achievements with, so I didn't really understand – but I could not have asked for a better baby. She was such a happy, undemanding child.

We had no sooner celebrated Sarah's first birthday than Trevor was offered a promotion which meant moving down to Hertfordshire. It was a huge upheaval leaving the area I'd grown up in and I'd never really been anywhere else, but it was exciting too. The last couple of years, Trevor had been employed as assistant plant engineer at ICI in the north-east, but now that ICI were setting up a cavity insulation business in the south, they wanted a manager for their new operation.

It was Trevor's first white-collar, managerial role and came with a decent salary and prospects. ICI treated us well and we lived rent-free for the first six months at Tewin Village, a lovely village just outside Welwyn Garden City. It was an affluent area with private schools, small independent shops and enormous houses with manicured lawns. I had never lived anywhere like this before and it was as different as it could be to where we lived in Thornaby. As soon as we got there and saw the place, Trevor and I thought we'd arrived! But we wanted our own place again and, realistically, even with Trevor's managerial salary, Tewin Village was completely out of our price range. So as soon as the sale of our property in Thornaby came through, we began house-hunting every weekend to find something to suit our little family, where Trevor could commute without too much difficulty to work. Eventually we found a lovely little semi with gardens back and front in the market town of St Neots, near Cambridge, and we settled in there. Within a year of moving, on 20 July 1973, our second child, Victoria Jane was born. Vicki was a beautiful baby with even more dark hair than Sarah. She was also harder work, which after having had it so easy with Sarah came as a shock! Still, Trevor took the week off to look after Sarah and to help out. Back then there was no such thing as paternity leave, so once Trevor went back to work, and with no family around for support, I had to get on with it.

A few days after Vicki was born, Trevor brought Sarah in to see her little sister for the first time. Because of the problems I'd had giving birth to Sarah, I had been put down for another C-section. After the birth, Vicki was placed in a cot by the side of my bed. 'This is your little sister,' we said to Sarah, 'come and say hello.' Sarah peered in at her, gave her a tickle and then turned to Trevor and said, 'Are we going now, Dad?' I laughed; she was completely disinterested.

'Do you want to help me bath Vicki?' I asked Sarah, trying to get her involved. 'We can take her for a walk in the pram after, if you like.'

Sarah would help for a little while, but she soon became bored and would instead go out to play in the garden or around at her little friends' houses.

Like every parent, our lives changed dramatically when we had children. Here we were with a new life in a different part of the country with these two beautiful little girls, and I could not have loved them any more than I did, and still do, or been any happier. They were the biggest and most important part of my life, and my family was complete.

Chapter 6

After settling into our new home, I soon made friends with other young mums in the area. Our children would often play out together in the safe, secluded close where we lived, and at other times Sarah and Vicki would happily play together on their own. As with any small children, the girls would squabble on occasion, but the house was always ringing with laughter. I became a stay-at-home mum, which was the norm, and I loved the quality time I got to spend with my daughters.

Sometimes Auntie Lizzie would ring to say she was coming to stay. She came down that first Christmas, intending to stay for a few days, but enjoyed it so much that she stayed for weeks at a time. She loved Sarah and Vicki, and of course they loved her and looked forward to all the treats she would bring them. She always brought her knitting needles with her too, and when the girls were babies she spent hours making them little jackets and bootees, just as she'd done for me when I was a child.

I loved Auntie Lizzie dearly and worried about her when she went home, as by now even Uncle Tommy had got married and gone, leaving Auntie rattling round in the old house all on her own, which I think she found difficult. In the end she decided to pack up and move into a small bungalow down the road that was better suited to her needs. I was pleased for her, but it was sad to think that the house at Coronation Crescent where I'd grown up and learned so much, and which had always been so busy and so full of life, was now empty and gone. But I didn't have time to dwell on it then, as I had my hands full looking after Trevor and the girls.

Trevor was a great help with Sarah and Vicki at weekends when they were little. He would change their nappies and read them a bedtime story and take them to the park to feed the ducks and play on the swings. He was a good dad. By the time Vicki was three and Sarah was six and attending the local infants' school, Trevor had decided it was time to move on with his career. He heard about a post as a project engineer with BOC in Hammersmith, applied straight away and got the job. I was delighted for him, but a daily commute from St Neots to West London wasn't going to be practical, so we had to sell the house and move to a large, 1930s three-bedroom semi in Pinner. I was so thrilled to be moving to London, it was the place I'd always dreamed of as a child as I'd watched the trains heading south across the Yarm viaduct. We used to watch from the playground at school as the 9 o'clock flyer to London shot by, and as a child it excited me that London was where the Queen lived. And now here I was, still in my twenties, living in a lovely house in a leafy suburb of London with my own little family; it was a dream come true.

When we lived in St Neots, Trevor had worked very long hours, only coming home at night when he'd finished all that he needed to do, and for a while he had spent two nights of the week working away from home. I began to call him a 'hunter-gatherer' as it became obvious to me that he always had his eye on a bigger salary and the next step up the career ladder. That changed for a little while after we moved to Pinner, when Trevor would come home every evening at six. I really liked having him home then, as it meant we could all sit down and eat together as a family. Then, later on in the evening when the girls were in bed, Trevor and I would sit and chat about our day and watch TV together, which hadn't happened in years. I loved him being in that job, but sadly it wasn't to last long. Trevor hated the daily commute and the regular hours. He wasn't a nine-to-six man and after six months of this cosy, domestic routine, his hours increased again, and he began spending two nights away every week, on a project in Bromborough on the Wirral, near to Liverpool. My hunter-gatherer was back out there, doing what he did best.

Because of all the time the girls and I were spending together, we developed a special bond between us. It was certainly a wrench when Vicki turned four and a half and started at the local Longfield school that Sarah was attending. I really missed the girls during the day and looked forward to picking them up after school and hearing what they'd done. I needed to get back to some kind of work, to fill in that time. I had too much time in the day without them.

One morning at the school gates the headmistress, Miss Perks, asked me how I was. I told her I was so bored without the girls at home, and she invited me to come and see her the next morning to talk about things I could do to help out at the school. I started volunteering that very week: making jam tarts and scones with the kids in cookery class. I loved how enthusiastic the children were! And soon I was volunteering two or three days a week. Sometimes I would sit with the remedial kids, helping them with their reading. It was a wonderful school, and I learned a lot about education there. It was my first job outside the home since having Sarah; my first step back out into the world of work.

It wasn't long after this that Trevor began working away again for two nights a week, so I was pleased when my brother David rang and asked if he could pop down for a few days. David was twenty-one by this time, and I was looking forward to seeing him.

'Of course,' I said, 'come and stay as long as you like.'

David took me at my word; he came intending to stay for the weekend but ended up living with us for the next six years. He got himself a job at Kodak, up the road in Harrow. Although he worked shifts, it was good to have family around and the girls loved his company.

'Can we play a game, Uncle David?' 'Can you take me on the swings, Uncle David? Please . . .' Poor David never got any peace!

On Sundays, the girls would go to Sunday school at the local Baptist Free church, which had ties to their school. Sarah and Vicki enjoyed going there, and I was fine with it, as it didn't have a 'holier than thou' ethos but taught the girls the importance of empathy and kindness, as their school did. There was a lot of clapping, singing and laughter there too, which is why I think the girls liked going. Sarah particularly enjoyed it, hearing all the parables of Jesus as I had done as a child. As she got older, she became a real

34

believer in the Church's interpretation of God and developed a strong social conscience.

Sarah was in middle school at Longfield and Vicki was in the first school there. The head of the lower school, Mr Brignall, was a lovely man who laid an amazing foundation for Vicki and Sarah's education. He based the school ethos on humanity and well-being as well as academic achievement, and the girls studied subjects such as French from seven years old and did very well there.

Vicki, who had only been at Longfield a short while, soon began to pick up on people's little idiosyncrasies. One day she came home from school and said to Sarah and me, 'I love it when Mr Brignall takes assembly.'

'What do you love about it?' I asked her.

'When we're singing hymns, you can hear him rattling the change in his coat pocket in time to the music,' she said.

She was so serious when she said it and had no idea how funny she sounded, but she made Sarah and me burst into laughter. Vicki loved the strangest things about people and was brilliant at observations and impressions. One minute she would be impersonating the head speaking to a teacher, the next she'd shift positions and reply as the teacher he was talking to. She'd really get it off pat. Sarah and I would be lying on the sofa in stitches, tears streaming down our faces. 'Stop it, Vicki, stop it!' we'd beg her, but she'd do it all the more until our sides felt as if they would split from laughing.

Sarah also had a fun and quirky take on life, so in that way my girls were alike. When she was eight, I picked her up after school one day and asked her, 'What did you do at school today, Sarah?'

'We played knicker chase,' she replied.

'Knicker chase? What's that?' I asked.

'We play it at lunchtimes, in the playground. The boys chase us and when they catch us, we have to show them our knickers,' she replied matter-of-factly.

'Oh dear,' I said, concerned. 'Would you like me to have a word with your teacher about it?'

'Oh no!' she said. 'I like it!'

One of the things my daughters and I always shared was a good sense of humour, and we always ended up laughing together – even though Vicki had no idea how funny she was.

With the girls settled into school, I started to look for a job which would fit around their hours and found a post at a private school in Pinner as a teaching assistant. I enjoyed working with the little ones in the kindergarten, and since I finished at three o'clock it meant I could be there to pick up the girls when they came out of school. I got all the school holidays off too and, with David helping out as needs be, life was pretty perfect.

Though Sarah didn't realise it at the time, she was exceptionally bright in every subject from a young age. She learned to play the cello at Longfield, even if her practising at home was excruciating to hear. Really there was nothing she could not do, but she was always an unassuming little girl, as well as a tomboy. She loved playing games with the boys and being out riding her bike, but she hated going to parties if it meant she had to wear a dress. When she was little, she wouldn't wear dresses at all if she could help it. Vicki, on the other hand, despite being of the opinion that boys were 'horrible, dirty stinky things', loved to wear nice dresses and clothes right from the off, and she very quickly became interested in fashion.

When Sarah was eight and Vicki turned five, I found a great opportunity to share my love of Liverpool FC with them. I was still an avid follower and knew they were due to play Arsenal in the Charity Shield final at Wembley Stadium, which was not far from where we lived. So I said to Trevor, 'Let's see if we can get tickets and take the girls to the game.'

Trevor didn't look particularly interested. He was worried that Vicki was too young to take to a match, but when I told David, he was totally up for it. In the end, Trevor relented and the five of us went. We bought flags for the girls outside the ground, but when Trevor got his wallet out to pay, the man at the ticket machine took one look at Vicki smiling up at him with her huge blue eyes and said, 'Oh, don't worry about paying for the little girl,' and he lifted Vicki over the turnstiles and handed her to me.

So there she was, a ticketless fan! As Vicki got older, she only had to look at people with her beautiful dark hair and those big blue eyes and she could wrap people round her little finger, especially my brother David.

The ground was packed with a crowd of 92,000 and all you could hear were the Liverpool and Arsenal fans trying to out-chant each other. The stadium was one great mass of red flags. We took our seats in the stand, where the girls could see. The fans who had travelled down from Liverpool were so friendly; there was such a lot of camaraderie and banter that it felt like we were all one big family. I guess that was what I was used to at home in Yarm, so I loved it at the game with all the other supporters.

Then came the crackle from the ground's speakers as the name of the players from both teams were called out, a huge roar going up as Liverpool's Phil Neal, Alan Kennedy, Phil Thompson, Ray Kennedy, Alan Hansen, Kenny Dalglish, Jimmy Case, David Johnson, Terry McDermott, Graeme Souness and Ray Clemence emerged from the tunnel. What icons of the team of 1979 they were!

The atmosphere at the match was amazing, but I remember looking down at the girls, worried they might be getting bored and fractious, prompting Trevor to say, 'See, I told you so.' But Sarah and Vicki just sat there wide-eyed, taking it all in. It seemed too good to be true, so I said to David, 'I can't see this lasting long, we'll maybe get to half-time if we're lucky.'

But when I asked Vicki if she was fed up, she said, 'No, Mummy, I like it!' And when the game started, they were both riveted.

After a brilliant goal by captain Terry McDermott, the half-time whistle blew. Vicki and Sarah couldn't wait for the game to restart and pestered me, wanting to know where the team had gone. In the second half both Dalglish and McDermott scored, making it 3-0, until Alan Sunderland managed a compensatory goal for the Gunners near the end. The final score was 3-1. What a victory! When the team picked up the Charity Shield and the fans burst into a proud but raucous 'You'll Never Walk Alone', it sent a shiver down my spine, and still does today – although with a different resonance now. Once the supporters began filing out, Sarah and Vicki were so in awe, they would have happily stayed. There was no doubt they'd got the Peat footballing bug!

A few seasons later, Trevor and the girls and I became season-ticket holders, and every Saturday when Liverpool were at home, we drove up to Anfield for the game and back home again afterwards. With Trevor working ever longer hours, it was one of the few times we were all together, so we made a family outing of it. Every Friday evening, I made us a picnic lunch for when we got there. But one of the most memorable parts for us all was when we went through those Anfield turnstiles, particularly for the first time. There was such an incredible atmosphere with a sea of red flags and scarves waving and a joyous fellowship between the fans – the girls revelled in it. They were also fascinated by the Kop, which is directly behind the goal at the home end, where a seething mass of 27,000 hard-core supporters stood every Saturday to worship the team they adored. But it would be a good many years before the girls would be old enough to stand there together.

We travelled to some of the away matches too and when we couldn't go for some reason, we'd watch the match results on TV. Over the months and years, we became seasoned Liverpool supporters. But it still haunts me to this day, the thought that if I hadn't introduced Sarah and Vicki to football and LFC, they would still be here with me now. It might not make much sense to others, but it is one of the hardest things I have had to come to terms with since the girls passed. And although I know they would not want me to think that, it is something that will always be with me.

★

As well as Saturdays being a family day out, we had great family holidays together too. On one occasion we rented a villa on the Tuscany coast and drove nearly the whole length of France, up into the mountains and through the Mont Blanc tunnel, to get there. Sarah was eleven by then and Vicki eight, and after having a fantastic two weeks there, instead of travelling the length of France to catch the ferry home, Trevor and I decided to drive back via Lake Como, Switzerland, Germany, France, Luxembourg and Belgium, en route to Calais. We stopped off in Brussels, and the girls were fascinated when they saw Manneken Pis, the bronze statue of the little boy relieving himself into the fountain basin. 'Mum, look he's got his willy out,' Sarah said, bemused, while Vicki, who didn't like boys at the time, promptly denounced it as 'Disgusting!'

Ironically, we had dropped down into Strasbourg before that, where I had asked the girls if they wouldn't mind standing outside the Court of Human Rights so that I could take their picture. So, my two little daughters stood there grinning as I took the snap. How poignant to think that had it not been for European Law and the Court of Human Rights, we would not have got a second inquest that was finally to be so important in all our years of campaigning for truth and justice after their deaths.

Chapter 7

Pinner was a wonderful area for the girls to grow up in. Vicki had ice skating lessons at Richmond ice rink every Saturday morning, which Trevor would take her to, while Sarah and I had a lie-in. Trevor and I also had a good social circle and during the summer when the football season was over, our friends Chris and Jeff from North Harrow would come over with their children at weekends.

After six years working at the kindergarten, I decided it was time to move on, so I got a full-time job at a local head office, doing clerical work again. It was a good company and they brought round coffee and biscuits in the morning and tea and biscuits in the afternoon. I remember thinking how much easier this was than staying at home! I couldn't have done it without David helping me out, being there when the girls came home from school and during the holidays.

Every June a fair came to Pinner, and set up in the High Street, with a big wheel and lots of stalls. All the children used to look forward to it. I'd started working full time by then, and asked my brother David if he could take the girls. Vicki begged him, 'Please, please, please, Uncle David, take us to Pinner Fair!' She was eight years old then and of course David couldn't refuse her a thing, so he took her to the fair, where she won a goldfish by throwing a ping-pong ball into a goldfish bowl. She brought the little fish home in a plastic bag and we put it in a large tank with ornaments and weed to make it as natural an environment as possible for the fish, with room to swim. But one morning, before Vicki got up for school, David found the poor little goldfish floating on its side. 'She is going to be so upset,' I said.

David replied, 'Don't let her see it. You get her off to school and I'll sort something out.'

David went down to the pet shop and got her a new one, but a year on that one died too, and he went back and got another one, and this happened several times, with Vicki never realising there had been at least six different fish in that tank. Then one morning, I got up and heard Sarah calling up the stairs, 'Vicki, your goldfish is dead!'

But actually, believing that the fish had had a happy and long life, Vicki took it quite well. So she put the little fish in a large Swan Vesta matchbox and organised a funeral for it in the back garden. Sarah made a cross for the grave, and we buried it under the magnolia tree, where a few years later it would be joined by Jemima and Sooty, the girls' pet rabbits.

Around this time, Sarah's best friend at school was taking the entrance exam for Haberdashers' Aske's School for Girls in Elstree. Sarah asked her about the school and, liking what she heard, asked me and her dad if she could take the entrance exam too. Trevor didn't know much about private schools, and the little I knew was limited to the school where I worked. However, after some research we found it not only had an excellent academic record but also had the same kind and caring ethos of Longfield school, and so we agreed she should take the exam. In all honesty, Sarah did not do much prep for it, but she was naturally extremely bright and passed with flying colours. It gave her confidence, knowing she had picked out the school for herself, and she had absolutely made the right choice. We were thrilled for Sarah and had a little celebration tea for her at the weekend.

Things were going well for Trevor too. He had moved into a higher-paid job again, still working in the City, still leaving home early in the morning and returning home whenever he'd satisfied those hunter-gatherer instincts of his. Occasionally, I would say to him, 'Trevor, I would love it if you could be home early tonight for a change, to have dinner with us.'

But Trevor's reply was always the same: 'Jenni, you live in cloud cuckoo land! If you wanted a nine-to-five man you should've married a factory worker and lived on his nine-to-five wages.'

I didn't like it, but because Trevor was so driven, he would never compromise on this issue. I had to admit he was a workaholic. I really don't think he could help it. As time went on and the girls got older, I let it drop and accepted this was how it was. He was never going to change.

Sarah loved it even more at Haberdashers' than she had anticipated and was getting on very well there. She was particularly good at maths and sciences, and took her maths, English and French O levels a year early, getting all A grades. It was hard for Vicki, following in the footsteps of her academically gifted sister, but Sarah never once boasted or rubbed her success in her face. Three years later, when Vicki was eleven, we gave her the same opportunity, and she surprised herself by getting into Haberdashers' too. That was great for Vicki, who was always measuring herself against her big sister and, in her own mind, falling short. It boosted her self-esteem, and it was good to have them both settled in the same school. After discussing it, Trevor and I felt it would be easier all round to move nearer to Haberdashers' for when Vicki started there. So we upped sticks again, moving to a large, four-bedroom detached house just down the road at Hatch End – and taking David with us too.

The house had lovely gardens front and back and was at the end of a quiet, tree-lined close. It was a great house for two growing young women, and they each had their own bedroom with a beautiful, shared Jack and Jill en suite. Life here was a completely different world to what I'd been used to as a young girl at Yarm, with a shared bedroom and one indoor bathroom, always with a queue outside. 'Aren't you out of there yet, Jennifer?' Uncle Tommy would yell, banging on the door. 'I'm desperate out here!'

Before we left Pinner, Vicki insisted on digging up the pets in our back garden to take to Hatch End. 'The goldfish and Jemima, and the others are all coming,' she said. She saw them as part of the family and wanted them to be with us. I could understand that, but in the end we managed to persuade her to take just the crosses from the graves, which we put out in the new garden!

We had been in our new home a year and Vicki had settled into her new school, when Trevor came home one evening quite excited.

'Great news!' he said. 'I've been offered the post of managing director of a company!' He was upbeat about it and what it would mean for his career, but when I asked him where it was based, I was stunned when he replied, 'Kingswinford, near Dudley in the West Midlands.'

I was lost for words for a moment. 'Well, it's great they recognised your talent and business acumen,' I eventually congratulated him. 'But you're not thinking of accepting it, are you? I mean, what about Sarah and Vicki?'

Sarah was at a critical stage of her A levels, so there was absolutely no way I could take her out of school to start all over again at a new school in another part of the country. Besides, she had friends at Habs and was happy there, and the same was true of Vicki, who was about to choose her GCSE courses. On that basis alone I wouldn't move the girls, so I said no and between us we agreed that I would stay in London and look after Sarah and Vicki and our home, while he rented a flat in Dudley and came home at weekends. We decided to wait and see how he settled into his job. It wasn't a perfect arrangement but at least the girls' education wouldn't suffer. So Trevor would go away at 5 a.m. every Monday and not return home again until late every Friday night. This would later change to Trevor going back on a Sunday afternoon so that he didn't have to get up early the next day.

In effect, I guess he had become a weekend dad while I was at home running the show. In his absence, the three of us soon settled into a routine with both girls becoming protective of me. Sarah was really practical and could change fuses, even when the dishwasher threw the electrics and we were left in the cold and dark. Vicki was like me, she

45

wouldn't touch wires and fuses, but Sarah always took charge. Vicki and I would stand back, and sometimes hold the stepladder. That was our role. By this point, David had moved out to live with his girlfriend, Dolores, so the girls and I really were a team during those years Trevor worked away, and we had some special times together.

At the weekend we had a different routine. On Fridays, I'd go shopping after work then cook the evening meal, which I'd have with the girls, and set aside a snack for Trevor when he arrived home later that night. Saturdays were full with going to watch Liverpool play, either home or away, which meant Sundays were filled with domestic chores, and cooking the Sunday roast. There was always lots of washing and ironing, including Trevor's, as he brought home his laundry. I remember Vicki saying one day as Trevor brought in his bag of washing, 'Don't they have any washing machines in Dudley then, Dad?'

I didn't think about it at the time but just accepted that this was how things were, but Vicki was quite right to question it, because I worked too.

Perhaps, with us being so close, it meant Trevor felt left out. In fact, he told me he sometimes felt like an intruder when he came home at the weekends. However, I guess this was inevitable as we were spending so much time apart. The girls had school and homework to do, I had a job to go to and a home to run; we all had busy lives. Sarah, Vicki and I worked well as a team during those times, and I'm sad that Trevor missed out on the years when the girls were growing into young women and all the memories we made together. I was the lucky one and blessed to have that precious time – I cherish those days and those memories.

Chapter 8

As Sarah and Vicki grew up, the similarities and differences between them became more apparent. While Sarah had sailed through the teenage years, Vicki was a typical teen and sometimes when I tried to speak to her she would give me this look and say, 'You love her better than me!' and rush out, slamming the door behind her. I think it was those rampant teenage hormones playing up. But for all that, Vicki still looked up to me. In fact, so much so that I used to say to her, 'Vicki, will you please take me down off that pedestal because if you don't, one day I am going to fall off!'

Though the girls shared an abiding love of LFC, they had very different personalities and interests, including their tastes in music. If Vicki was playing Culture Club and Sarah put on The Cure or Bowie, Vicki would turn up the volume, which only meant one thing – Sarah would blast hers out to outdo her sister. In the end I would have to yell up the stairs, 'The man eight doors down just said, can you please turn that music down! He can't hear himself think!'

It was the usual sibling rivalry stuff, but they also did things together. Every Thursday afternoon when Habs finished for the day, Sarah and Vicki would head off to the local riding school. Sarah had taken riding lessons first, then

Vicki decided she'd like to go too, but she wanted me and Trevor to buy her a beautiful but expensive pair of fitted leather riding boots. The kind that look good even when you're not going anywhere near a horse.

'Oh, don't worry about getting new riding boots,' Sarah advised her. 'They let you wear wellies if you're new.'

And I got Sarah's point – it wasn't as if they were going showjumping; they were only learning to ride. Sarah was quite happy to hire a hat and wear the wellingtons the riding school provided, and we certainly didn't want to waste money, so I said to Vicki, 'Are you sure you want to go to riding school?'

'Oh, yes,' she said. 'I want to do the same as Sarah.'

'But are you certain you're going to like riding?' Trevor asked her.

'Of course I am,' Vicki replied. 'But I'm not wearing wellies and hats that other people have worn! That is gross!' she complained, which was so typical of her.

So, Trevor and I forked out for her brand-new riding boots, leather crop and hat, and off she went to the first lesson. But soon after, I got the impression she wasn't so keen to go as she had been, so I said to Sarah, who was in the same class, 'I'm not sure Vicki really likes riding.'

'God no,' Sarah replied, 'she hates it!'

'Hates it?'

'You want to see her when we all go round in a circle on our horses – she looks ridiculous in all that professional riding gear, and she won't even pull up the reins because she doesn't want to hurt the horse's mouth.'

'Well, I get that, that's nice,' I said.

'Well, yes, so do I,' Sarah replied. 'But Vicki just sits there with the reins hanging down, complaining about the horse in front having wind all the time.'

Wind? I hadn't expected it to be about that! So that evening I asked Vicki, 'What's going on at the riding school?'

'It's Snowball,' she said, 'the horse that walks round in front of my mine. It keeps lifting its tail and farting in my direction, and I hate it!'

Vicki was so outraged that she had me and Sarah in stitches once again, though as usual she had no idea why. She hadn't dared tell me and Trevor that she hated riding because of what we'd spent on her outfit, so she'd just kept on going. In the end we sold her riding kit, though she kept the riding boots which looked so stylish on her.

After Sarah turned sixteen, she took a further ten O levels that summer and got A grades for all of them, which was the highest you could get at that time. But Sarah played down her success, as she had when she'd got into Habs. Mobile phones did not exist then, only landlines, so when her school friends rang her that morning to compare their results, I heard her in the hall quietly fobbing them off with, 'Oh, I did OK,' before hanging up. When she saw me standing there, she looked really worried.

'Mum,' she said, 'please don't tell anyone I've got all A grades.'

Now if it had been Vicki that had got those results, she'd have had hired the Red Arrows to fly over with a banner saying, 'Vicki Hicks got ten A grades!' But here was Sarah, who did not have a competitive bone in her body, pleading with me to keep her success quiet. It was one of the biggest differences between them.

Despite Sarah's pleas, I was bursting to tell the world and his dog. How I managed not to, I really don't know. Though since Sarah passed away, I have told anyone and everyone, including the press and interviewers on TV – anyone who would listen to me – 'Sarah got ten As at O level, you know,' adding, 'and three grade As in French, English and maths, which she took a year earlier, when she was only fifteen!'

I sometimes imagine Sarah, wherever she is, saying, 'Mum! I told you not to say anything!'

Little did she know that Vicki, who was so proud of her sister, had already spilled the beans to her classmates. Then, much to Sarah's chagrin, when the results were about to be read out in assembly, Vicki's mates, who knew what was coming, started cheering and shouting. As Vicki said to me, 'You should have seen Sarah at school today, she went bright red on that stage.'

Sarah didn't like a big fuss about things like that; she was modest and shy and found it embarrassing that she excelled at whatever she turned her hand to.

Sarah continued to attend the local Baptist Free Church in North Harrow. She would meet her friends there every Sunday evening and loved the message of love and caring for others that she heard there. It appealed to her own sensibilities and her desire to help others, so I wasn't surprised when she said she wanted to be baptised. I decided to support her by joining her in an Emerson baptism, which is a ceremony where you are totally immersed in water.

Sarah hoped Trevor and Vicki would agree to be baptised too, but they were both against the idea, though Trevor did agree to come and watch. Vicki didn't want to come, but I didn't give her a choice. She'd already fallen out with the Sunday school the year before when she'd turned up one morning in a short skirt. This did not go down well with the Sunday school teacher who, much to Vicki's disgust, told her to come in something longer next time. Vicki's answer to that was, 'Well, if God doesn't like me because of my clothes, I'm not going to church any more!'

That was my youngest daughter, and that was the end of that!

The baptism service was scheduled for Sunday, 29 June, which was the same evening as the World Cup Final was on TV. Argentina were playing West Germany and Vicki, who never missed a World Cup Final, wasn't about to miss this one. She'd seen Diego Maradona's infamous 'Hand of God' incident in the quarter-finals that had led to Argentina beating England 2–1 and knocking us out of the tournament. Vicki called him a cheat and wanted West Germany to win because of it. She sat at the back of the church by the door with her earpiece in, listening to the match on the radio. Sarah and I couldn't see her from where we were, but Vicki mustn't have been pleased when West Germany lost 3-2, although Sarah was undoubtedly happy that her sister was there to support her.

Sarah was concerned for others and was becoming increasingly aware that there were others less fortunate than herself.

'I know *I* went to a good school, but all children should have access to the same quality of education as I have

– money shouldn't come into it,' she said to me one day, hating the injustice that her privilege afforded her a good education, but not others.

She told me she had been on the top deck of the uni bus, which ran from the halls of residence and passed through a run-down area of Liverpool where some children were out playing.

'They are never going to have the same opportunities I've had,' she said, 'but they are just as clever as me and anyone else.'

I thought she had a fair point, but she and Trevor would often clash over their polarised views. Trevor had private healthcare insurance with BUPA through his job, which meant if we had any problems, we could head off up the road to a new private hospital at Bushey. I had been to my GP for a medical check, as had Vicki, who had a problem with pain in her knee. My GP wanted some thickening in my breast checked and asked if I had any private health cover. I said I had, so he telephoned the BUPA hospital and got us straight in that afternoon. Sarah came with us. When we arrived, we found the hospital was set among tall trees in lovely grounds.

Vicki got out of the car. 'Come on then,' she said, 'let's get in there!' But Sarah refused.

'No, I'm not going in!' she announced. 'Private health services should not exist in this country when we have the NHS!'

She was adamant she wasn't going to set foot in the building, so she waited for us outside in the car. Vicki, on the other hand, loved the look of the modern building and could not wait to go in. As soon as she'd been seen by the consultant, she came running out, telling Sarah, 'It's like a five-star hotel in there! They even bring you tea and coffee while you wait! With biscuits!'

But Sarah was disappointed in us. 'You two should be ashamed of yourselves!' she said. 'Going in those places and taking doctors away from their real work in the NHS!'

Oh, we got another lecture from Sarah, Vicki sitting quietly in the back of the car. Sarah, however, had a valid point and I began to see that more clearly when she was no longer with us, when her sense of social injustice would become mine.

Vicki was very different to Sarah in that way. Her ambition from a young age had been to own a black Porsche or a red Ferrari, which Sarah would have laughed at. Vicki loved the look of those cars. She worked hard at school and at home to earn money, because I brought her up with the principle that if you wanted to get on in life, that's what you had to do. But to be fair to Vicki, she would never see anyone down without trying to help them – although she would prefer to do it in expensive designer clothes and shoes for which she saved up all her pocket money! That was so typical of Vicki, who, by her mid-teens, would save up and get knitwear from Stefano's, an Italian designer shop on Oxford Street. Sarah would have looked stylish in a binbag and dressed like your average student in casual clothes and DM boots, usually with her hair casually swept up. She was five foot eight and a size 10, with very long legs. I don't know where she got her model height from, because Trevor is only five foot eight and I barely make it to five foot. If we were both standing up, I would have to crane my neck if I spoke to her and would sometimes joke with her, 'Sit down while I'm telling you off, Sarah, because you're hurting my neck!'

Vicki was smaller at five foot three, but she was still taller than me. She was always immaculately tidy. You would open her drawers to find she had colour-coordinated all her socks with her underwear. By contrast, if Sarah took anything off, she would chuck it down anywhere. Her room always looked like a bomb had gone off, and when Vicki discovered she'd been in her room, she'd get cross at her: 'If you are going to come in here when I'm out, don't touch anything on my dressing table because I've set everything out and I don't want you making a mess of it!'

I'd have to play referee between them, but they would always end up as friends. Nothing but nothing could break that bond between them; they were fiercely loyal to each other and had each other's back right up until the end.

Chapter 9

A year before the match at Hillsborough, when Sarah was coming up to taking her A-level exams, I started a job as a technician in the earth sciences department at a sixth-form college in Stanmore. The college took in some young people who had failed their GCSEs first time round and needed to retake them before going on to do A levels. I loved the job, which involved preparing soil samples, ensuring all the written notes were in order and assisting the students whenever they needed a hand.

The job started at nine in the morning, which meant I had to be well-organised at home to make sure I got there on time, and got Vicki to school on time too. In the evenings I did all the cooking but, during the holidays, Sarah and Vicki would help out. Sarah made the best prawn-cocktail sauce and vegetarian stir-fry I have ever tasted. It was delicious. Her secret ingredient was adding lots of Cointreau! Vicki was particularly good at desserts and baking, so with the two of them, it was a winning combination.

At weekends, the girls and I would sprawl out on the huge sofa in the lounge, chatting and laughing and watching TV together. But I will always remember one particular evening when Sarah was upstairs studying and Vicki and I were relaxing on the sofa, she suddenly blurted out, 'Mum, we're like a one-parent family, aren't we?'

I was shocked and replied, 'Vicki, don't let your dad hear you say that! He wouldn't like it!'

But she gave me a look as if to say, *Well, he's not going to hear me say it, because he's not here, is he?*

I was sorry that Trevor missed so much of that time when the girls were growing into young women. But as I explained to Vicki, her dad had to work the same as I did, so that we could live the way we did, in this lovely house and beautiful area. I think she accepted that.

Because of how caring Sarah had been as a child, Trevor and I weren't surprised when she announced one day that she wanted to go into medicine. In fact, we were both convinced she would have ended up helping the sick and disabled in a developing country. So, when the time came for A-level students at her school to start applying to universities, I took her to a careers evening at Habs where they had presentations from London teaching hospitals. Sarah spoke to several doctors from these hospitals, who were all saying to her, 'Yes, we want you at our hospital.'

I was really excited about it and said to her, 'Sarah, all these teaching hospitals want you! What an amazing opportunity!'

She turned to me and, looking very serious, replied, 'Mum, I don't know how to tell you this, but I don't want to be a doctor any more.'

I was surprised and asked her, 'Why, Sarah, what on earth has made you change your mind?'

'It's the thought of all that blood, Mum. I'm too squeamish.'

After looking at the leaflets on display and speaking to the medics, she'd suddenly realised this wasn't the career for her. In fact, Sarah wasn't sure what she wanted to study at university but finally she decided to apply to do chemistry, which was a subject that came naturally to her. Having got the A-level results she needed, we were thrilled when she was given the opportunity of a place at Oxford University and also Imperial College London, with a full scholarship, but as usual she played down her success and didn't seem to be particularly interested in either of them.

Then it dawned on me that Sarah had also applied to Liverpool University as one of her choices, and I realised this was where she'd wanted to go all along. She wanted to study in the city where her heart was, and her beloved Anfield. I think she hadn't articulated that to us as she was worried about the reaction she would get. Her turning down the opportunity to go to Oxford was a huge disappointment for Trevor, but at the end of the day we just wanted to make sure Sarah was making the right choice for herself.

It turned out that we were not the only ones worried for her. Her grades all exceeded what Liverpool University required, but when she accepted their offer of a place at the interview, they asked her to give it some thought: was she really sure about it? I thought that was good of them. Sarah said she was absolutely certain and wrote to Oxford to say she'd found a university where she thought she would be really happy. She was relieved to have made her decision, but on the Monday morning she was called in to the head's office at Habs and asked to explain why she had turned down two excellent offers. A student getting a place at Oxford or Cambridge was a feather in the school's cap too and I expect they were not pleased about her choice, but in hindsight I think it was very brave of Sarah to go through with what she wanted to do, rather than to go along with what was expected of her. As it turned out, we'll never know.

Sarah went up to university in the autumn of 1988. It was a Thursday and we had to get her there for her first day in the student halls of residence. When we arrived, there were dozens of other parents taking in boxes and cases from their cars for their children. I hadn't been to university myself at that time, so I didn't know what to expect, but I was so pleased at how appealing the Carnatic Halls of Residence were. She was allocated room D17, which was a lovely space, and there were all these other young freshers around everywhere. It made me feel confident that Sarah would be safe there.

We had been planning and shopping for a few weeks, buying the stuff Sarah would need for her new room: a duvet, bedding and towels, all the things to make her room comfortable. The day before, we bought lots of food at Waitrose to make sure she wouldn't starve. Every time when we went up to see her after that, I'd do a food shop for her. Trevor would give me this look as if to say, 'You know she's not going to starve away from home?' Maybe I was being overly concerned, as her university friends later told me the cupboard in her room was always so full it began to look more like a mini shop!

Sarah got cold feet a few days before going and so I had to be brave and over-the-top positive to help her see what an incredible opportunity it was. I won't pretend it wasn't hard when I said goodbye to Sarah that first time after dropping her off – it was my first child leaving home – but at the same time this was her first step towards independence. I knew I would miss her terribly, but I also felt this was the place she wanted to be and I was happy for her, as much as I felt I'd left a piece of my heart with her. When we said our goodbyes, I just gave her a big hug and got in the car.

As we were driving home, I turned to Trevor and said, 'Isn't it brilliant that she's got all of that at the uni?'

Trevor looked at me a bit puzzled and said, 'You know, I'd been expecting to have a few problems with you after dropping her off.'

He knew how close we were and he told me he was so proud of how I'd handled it. We drove for an hour and a half, and then Trevor pulled in at a service station on the M6 while I stayed in the car. As soon as he'd gone, I burst into tears. I was beside myself, sobbing and inconsolable. When he came back, Trevor thought something terrible had happened in his absence.

'What's wrong, Jenni? What's going on?' I told him I was missing Sarah already and he said, 'Ah, I thought you were doing too well.'

I cried from those services all the way back to London that evening, even though we were coming back to see her two days later on the Saturday to take her to the match at Anfield!

We had been coming up as a family to watch Liverpool play for years by this time and the plan was to continue to do so now Sarah was here. We always arrived at Anfield early, as Vicki and Sarah liked to be there by one o'clock for the build-up. Trevor and I used to sit in the car park in Stanley Park first listening to Radio City, and at about two o'clock we would walk round and take our seats in the stadium. After the game, we'd have a McDonald's before dropping Sarah off at halls, then the three of us would head home to London.

As soon as we got back, the TV would go on just in time to watch *Match of the Day*. Vicki had decided she wanted to become a sports journalist at this time, and on Sunday mornings she would get out an old typewriter I'd given her and write up the latest match report in her bedroom.

'Can I read one when you're finished?' I called up to her one day.

'No!' she shouted back. 'And don't you go looking for them either!'

'But how are you going to be a match reporter if you won't show anyone what you've written?' I asked her, because as soon as she'd finished the latest one, she'd hide it away in her bedroom with all the others. I don't know if she was shy about them, but they were always off limits!

On one occasion in the car park after a game at Anfield where Newcastle United, who happened to be my brother David's team, had beaten us, Vicki was so upset she refused to get in the car with her uncle David.

'I am not getting in that car with a person whose team beat us!' she insisted, digging in her heels. 'The ref was biased!' she scoffed.

I particularly remember how upset Vicki was at the 1988 FA Cup Final. It was the last game me and the girls ever went to together at Wembley. Liverpool were playing underdogs Wimbledon, and commentator John Motson dubbed the match on air as *Culture Club vs the Crazy Gang* and made us all laugh. But things didn't go well for Liverpool and shortly before half-time a Lawrie Sanchez header off a free-kick by Dennis Wise gave Wimbledon a 1-0 lead, and they then took control of the game for most of the second half. Seeing Princess Diana hand out the cup to the Wimbledon captain Dave Beasant and his holding it up at the end was all too much for Vicki, who was beside herself before we even got home. She was so competitive in everything she did herself, she simply couldn't accept it when her team lost. And in her match reports, Liverpool were never at fault. It was always the referee or the linesman who had missed something or were biased. One described a match on 11 October 1986, when she was fourteen:

> Liverpool 0 Spurs 1, Liverpool's Steve McMahon had an especially good game with many shots and good passes from start to finish. One shot in particular was pure brilliance. It was a full-blooded shot that had so much power in it that it half knocked Clemence over.

As Steve McMahon said in his autobiography, 'Not bad considering we lost!'*

*

---

* *Macca Can! The Steve McMahon Story* with Harry Harris, Pelham Books, London 1990.

With Sarah away at university, it was only me and Vicki at home and we missed her so much. However, she would call every evening before we ate. I used to buy her phonecards and she would ring from the payphone on the landing in the halls of residence. Sarah was full of it right from the start, telling Vicki and me all about the new friends she'd made, particularly Mark, Steve, Sharla and Rebecca. We heard stories about them dressing up for Halloween and their other antics – she was clearly having a ball!

When she came home for that last Christmas, we had a lovely time together. Trevor and I brought her an iconic, antique leather flying jacket like the one Kelly McGillis wore in *Top Gun*. She wore it with her Levi 501s and DMs. It looked great and she loved it so much she rarely took it off all the holidays, and wore it to return to university.

One Sunday afternoon in January, during the Christmas holidays, Trevor and I had one of those arguments over nothing which always seemed to come right after we'd had Sunday lunch. He would storm off upstairs, pack his bags and drive back to Dudley. It seemed to me like he was looking for an excuse to go. It was sad the weekend had to end like that.

I never knew where these arguments came from. After he left, I felt sad and upset and went upstairs. Sarah's door was open, and she was lying on her bed with her hands behind her head, watching TV. Realising she'd heard the argument, I tried to blink back the tears.

She wondered why her dad always went back to Dudley early, instead of spending more time with us.

'When I ring him from the halls of residence in the evening, whatever time it is, he's never in.'

I found myself defending Trevor: 'He has to go to business dinners in the evening, he has meetings and he's made friends up there.'

She looked at me and said nothing further. I closed the bedroom door so Vicki didn't hear – I didn't want her to hear, because I knew Vicki would challenge her dad about his whereabouts. I didn't really think about it again, Sarah returned to university, I went back to work, and life went on. We had the Easter holidays, and then Hillsborough. Looking back, Sarah was always an old head on young shoulders while in some ways perhaps I was naive.

By the time it was Vicki's turn to make her A-level choices, she and I went on our own to the school, as Trevor had a business meeting in Kingswinford. Like many other academic institutions, if Haberdashers' didn't think you were going to get an A grade in a subject, they wouldn't let you take it. But every teacher we spoke to said the same thing: 'Vicki, you are quite capable of doing this subject, so if you want to do it, great, we'll put you down for it.'

I was so impressed, and Vicki was delighted. Then we came to Mrs Wood, the geography teacher who had taught Sarah at O level but not at A level, as Sarah didn't get to take that one. So, we sat down with Mrs Wood, who told her, 'You've got to do A-level geography, Vicki, because the last person I had in my form who was as good as you went on to Cambridge.'

Things changed with Vicki from that moment. She had seen her big sister get into all these top universities and thought it wasn't going to happen to her. Now here was a teacher telling her she was capable of going to Cambridge.

I saw my youngest daughter grow that evening – she came out of the school a foot taller! Not least because Mrs Wood had taught Sarah too. Sadly, Vicki would not get to take her GCSEs or her A levels, but it did wonders for her confidence at the time and was amazing to see.

Sarah came home during the long Easter break in 1989, while I was on holiday from my new job at the sixth-form college. Vicki still had another week to go at school, so Sarah and I got to spend several days alone in each other's company. We spent the time doing all the simple things together, like shopping and cooking and doing the *Guardian* crossword – well, Sarah did it while I attempted to! We also discussed the books we liked. Sarah absolutely loved *To Kill a Mocking Bird* by Harper Lee, and George Orwell's *Animal Farm,* both of which she'd read at school for her English literature O level.

'Have you read *Animal Farm* yet?' she asked me as she leafed through the vegetarian cookbook I'd bought her for Christmas.

'Not yet,' I replied sheepishly. 'I've not had the time.'

'Mum, you've had them since I was fourteen!' she complained.

So I promised her I would read them as soon as I could, though with always being so busy I had no idea when that might be, and the books stayed on her shelf for quite some while. But how I treasure those days I spent with Sarah during that Easter break, because just three weeks' later, when Liverpool would be playing Nottingham Forest in the semi-final of the FA Cup at the Hillsborough Stadium, she would be gone.

The strange thing was that, when Sarah had first arrived home, I'd thought she seemed quieter than usual and I wondered if something might be worrying her. I knew she felt conflicted over two boys at uni who she really liked, so I said to her, 'You can talk to me, Sarah. You may not think it, but I was your age once. Nothing you can say will shock me.'

But she just looked at me over her coffee cup and said matter-of-factly, 'Mum, I don't want to carry on with my chemistry degree.'

I was taken aback for a moment, but I wasn't surprised. 'You don't? Why not?' I asked her.

'Oh my God,' she replied, 'it is just so easy.'

Yep, I thought to myself, *I knew it!* I'd told her so when she'd first decided to go for that subject. Sarah had never found chemistry challenging, and that was the problem. She was so gifted at it she was bored because it didn't stretch her.

'I can't work in a lab all day, Mum,' she went on. 'I admire people who can, but it's just not me.'

Another big part of Sarah's problem was that she could have done anything she wanted, but she didn't know what that was. As well as the sciences, she was very good at art and was therefore spoilt for choice.

'Look,' I said to her, 'you really need to make your mind up what you want to do, but don't go throwing three years of your life away on a chemistry degree if your heart's not in it. You need to think about what you want to do next.'

'I have thought about it, Mum,' she said. 'I've decided I want to do architecture.'

Architecture? She must have seen the look on my face.

'The thing is, I want to combine my artistic side with my science side, and this would be perfect.'

66

I thought about it a moment. 'Well, now you put it like that,' I said, seeing the sense in it.

Because Sarah loved being in Liverpool, I knew that whatever she chose to do next would involve her staying there. And sure enough, she told me that they had an excellent architecture department at the university, which she'd already checked out.

'Good,' I said. 'When you go back to uni after the Easter holidays, start making inquiries about switching your degree, because architecture is like training to be a doctor – it's going to take seven or eight years.'

She smiled, relieved that I approved. She might well have made a fine architect; however, we never got the chance to find out.

If Vicki was surprised to learn Sarah wanted to change her course, she didn't say so. I suspect she already knew. She had gone up to stay with Sarah the weekend before the Easter break, where she'd had Sarah's friends laughing at her impressions. Trevor and I had first become aware of her how good she was at it when she was about five and we had taken her to visit our friends in Wolverhampton. She might only have been little, but within a short space of time of us being there, she began speaking in a broad Wolverhampton accent. My friend was quite put out about it and said, 'Is she being funny or what?'

'No, she thinks it's polite that she speaks like the people that she's with. She thinks it's good manners.'

And she really did. When we became season-ticket holders, every time we went to Anfield her dad and I would sit in the main stand, and the girls would go and stand on the Kop. They were old enough now to have standing season tickets.

Sarah would say, 'You should be with her on the Kop, Mum – she starts speaking in a Scouse accent!'

She wasn't being rude or patronising, it was simply that in Vicki's world she felt everyone should do their best to fit in, that it would make everyone feel more comfortable – and she was so innocent about it.

When Vicki and I were on our own during the week, we would occasionally go to the cinema together, and during that last holiday when *Rain Man* was on in Harrow, I knew she would want to go. Although Vicki's favourite player was Steve McMahon at the time, she adored Tom Cruise and had posters of him all over her walls. So off we went to the cinema. It was to be the last film I would ever see with Vicki. I have watched that film so many times since then. Hundreds of times, in fact. If it's on television, I always have to watch it, as it reminds me of those last happy days we spent together.

During that Easter break before the Hillsborough game, Vicki, Sarah and myself were curled up on the sofa after dinner one night, chatting away, when a documentary came on the TV about cremation, of all things. I told them, all very tongue in cheek, 'Don't you two think of throwing me into some old furnace when I go. I want to be buried where you can come and visit me every week.'

'No, Mum,' Sarah replied, 'it will be you who will have to come and visit me.'

'Sarah!' I said. 'Let's not talk about that now. It's a long way off!'

'No. No, it's not, Mum.' And she said it so calmly that Vicki and I stared at her open-mouthed.

Then I said, 'Oh, Sarah, stop it! I was only messing about. I don't like this. You're frightening me now.'

'No,' she insisted, 'you are going to have to see to me.' Then she told me what she wanted played at her funeral: U2's 'With or Without You' from the *Joshua Tree* album that she'd asked us to get her for her birthday, which was only a few days away.

Vicki was upset too. 'We're not listening to any more of this, Sarah!' she said, and in an attempt to stop the conversation, she and I went through to the kitchen to warm up some milk to make hot chocolate. But Sarah followed us, still carrying on with it.

'And remember, Mum, I don't want any tears, because you have given me the happiest life I could have had. I could not have had a better life if I had picked it myself.'

It was too much for Vicki, who stormed off upstairs.

'I've heard enough of this now! I'm going to have a shower. When she shuts up talking like that, give me a shout, Mum, and I'll come back down!'

But still Sarah persisted: 'It's been a brilliant life, Mum, so no tears.'

I didn't like this conversation at all, it gave me nightmares even thinking about it, and it still does to this day.

I kept mulling it over, but I didn't tell her dad as I knew he would simply dismiss it as 'teenage nonsense'.

But there was something about the way Sarah said it that I believe she felt she had to get it out, to let me know. And that was just two weeks before Hillsborough.

Chapter 10

It was the day of the match, and we got up early to set off for our family day out.

With the girls' LFC scarves flying in the breeze from the back windows, we hit the M1 to Sheffield. At Junction 25, we were joined by Nottingham Forest supporters going up to the match, who beeped us as we passed each other on the way up. It was all good-natured fun, while inside the car we laughed and chatted away about who we thought would score for Liverpool, and planned our next trip to Wembley, as we were so confident we were going to win. Not least because we'd played the exact same semi-final fixture the previous year when we'd beaten Notts Forest 2-1, with Aldo (John Aldridge) scoring both goals. But it was also because we never doubted LFC would win; they were our team and, as the girls had said since they were little, 'Liverpool are the greatest!'

During the journey, Trevor mentioned renewing our season tickets for the next season and Sarah immediately replied, 'Oh yeah, I would still love mine.'

We naturally assumed Vicki would want to as well, when she unexpectedly announced, 'No, I don't think I will – I'm going to start a Saturday job.'

She told us it was in a shop called Zoo, a lovely little boutique in Harrow selling gorgeous clothes. I actually thought it would be an ideal job for Vicki, but I was surprised she was prepared to give up travelling to the matches. Looking back now, I see such an irony in that.

After Vicki's bombshell, I said to Trevor, 'Well, I'm seriously thinking about not renewing my season ticket either then. It's Vicki's first job and I want somebody to be there when she comes home.'

'Oh, for goodness' sake!' Trevor replied. 'She can have her own key for when she gets home, and she'll only be on her own for a few hours before we get back.'

I think Trevor thought I mollycoddled the girls, and I'm sure I did, but I couldn't help worrying about them. I wanted to make sure they were OK. That had always been my job. But I was so surprised that Vicki wouldn't be coming with us to see LFC play again, given that she was such a staunch Liverpool fan. Clearly, earning money was beginning to take the edge over the football, and she wanted that Ferrari!

We arrived at the same parking place close to the stadium that we'd been to once before, for the semi-final the year before. It was a lovely bright sunny day and warm too. We ate our picnic lunch in the car, but I kept back some cheese and pickle sandwiches I'd made for Vicki, as she'd always get hungry on the way home and they were her favourite. When we got to the area outside the ground there was a lot of camaraderie with the Notts Forest fans and soon we were all laughing and joking together about who was going to win. Then the four of us walked round towards the Leppings Lane end. It didn't take us as long this year, as the streets around the ground weren't cordoned off, nor were our tickets checked by police, as they had been the year before. Trevor had applied for our tickets through the season-ticket holders' ballot at LFC but, unfortunately, we were allocated three tickets for the standing area and another for the North Stand seated area. So, Trevor and I were to be split up again, just as we had been when we'd attended the 1988 semi-final, the previous year.

When we came to the Leppings Lane end we were over an hour early, so the turnstiles were relatively quiet. Despite the huge number of supporters that Liverpool had compared to Nottingham Forest, it was déjà vu as the Liverpool fans were once again given the smaller end of the ground with very few turnstiles. I remember thinking it was odd, but I didn't doubt that the police and security staff must know what they were doing so I didn't give it another thought. I knew Trevor would have preferred the seated ticket and I was happy to stand on the terraces with Sarah and Vicki, but the girls thought I'd have a better view in the seats because of my height,

'No, Mum, don't come in the standing area, you're far too small!' 'You won't see anything from there!' they insisted.

In the end I took the ticket for the seated area in the adjacent North Stand. I have no doubt the girls saved my life that day. They were my guardian angels, and I often think of that.

At the Leppings Lane turnstiles I hugged the girls and told them 'I love you', and we arranged to meet after the game at quarter to five, in the doorway of a little tobacconist shop on the corner near the Leppings Lane turnstiles entrance. Trevor and the girls then went their way and I went mine. I really wasn't too pleased at the prospect of sitting on my own again, when I heard a voice behind me shout, 'Mum!' I turned around and there was Vicki running towards me. She had picked up that I wasn't happy and gave me an extra big hug and kiss. Vicki told me she loved me, and then she was gone. And that would be the last time I would see my youngest daughter alive.

I took my seat in the North Stand at around ten to two. I don't remember much about the ground itself – I'd been to lots of football grounds all over the country and Hillsborough was not unusual. As I looked across the ground, the first thing I noticed was how sparsely filled the Leppings Lane end terraces were on either side, but how the middle area was really beginning to fill up. What I didn't realise then was that the middle sections were actually pens or metal cages; from where I was sitting, I just thought it was one large open terrace like the Kop at Anfield. At 2.15 I've since been told there came a tannoy announcement, asking fans in pens 3 and 4 to move forward to make room for others, but I don't recall hearing it. I couldn't understand why everyone was standing in the middle and not moving to the sides.

Bruce Grobbelaar, the goalie, later said that he'd noticed the same during the pre-match kick-around, at about 2.30, and wondered why the crowd weren't spreading into the empty areas at either end.

I looked to the left of me, which was the other end of the ground where the Forest fans were standing. It looked how I would have expected: there were scores of their supporters standing there but, being an open terrace, they were evenly spread across it and that's how the Leppings Lane end should have looked too. Where I was in the North Stand remained fairly empty and at quarter to three, when most football grounds start to fill up, I looked over again at the Liverpool fans. There was so much space on the terraces at either side of the central pens, while the middle area of the terrace just kept on filling up. Filling up. It had been packed in there at the semi-final the year before, but it was nothing like this. I was becoming seriously alarmed and kept thinking, *I hope to God Trevor and the girls aren't in the middle.*

I had assumed they would be standing together as they had been the year before, and turned to a stranger sitting near me and asked him, 'Does that look right to you? Because it doesn't look right to me.' They were packed in like sardines and still more were coming.

'There is loads of room at the side terraces,' I pointed out, 'but none in the middle.'

He nodded but seemed less concerned than me, and I wondered why the fans weren't being filtered to those areas.

As I watched those pens become even more tightly packed, I prayed to God again that Sarah and Vicki and Trevor weren't in there, and kept asking myself, *Why isn't something being done?*

Of course I had no idea about the horrendously ill-judged decision made by newly appointed match commander Chief Superintendent David Duckenfield at the time. All I knew was that there were dozens of fans desperately trying to climb out of the pens behind the goal. I was worried sick.

74

The game hadn't even kicked off yet, and the police were now physically pushing supporters back into what seemed to me to be quite obviously overcrowded pens. Some fans were making it over to the perimeter track, but not one of them ran onto the pitch, so it was certainly not a pitch invasion. A ground or track invasion, yes, but despite the fans' distress, even then they were respectful of the game about to be played.

The strange thing is, normally when the Liverpool team run out onto the pitch, and especially at a cup semi-final, we'd all be cheering the players and singing a deafening, 'You'll Never Walk Alone'. But because of what was unfolding in front of my eyes, I don't remember any of that, or even the referee blowing the whistle at 3 p.m., but he must have done as the game was now on. I'd been to so many football matches over the years that I knew this wasn't right, though if anyone else around me was worried, given the anxious state I was in, I didn't notice. I was desperately trying not to panic; however, it was obvious there was something very wrong happening on the Leppings Lane terrace.

Supporters in the upper terraces were now pulling fans up to safety from the pens below, as the police kept pushing back others who were attempting to jump on the track. Then a chap came running up the steps and called out to his friend behind me, 'There are dead people down there!'

I thought, I can't allow myself to believe what this man is saying, and I took a deep breath and repeated to myself, 'He's got to have it wrong. It's got to be OK.'

However, I was not aware that as early as 2.40 the fans in the pens had been chanting 'No more room! No more room!' to try to alert the authorities to their situation. Nobody listened, and nothing was done about it.

By 3 p.m., when the match started, another two thousand people had already been allowed to enter those pens. And with the uproar of the crowd getting behind their teams, I couldn't hear that behind the goal, the supporters were screaming at the Liverpool goalkeeper, 'Help us, Brucie! Help us! There are people dying in here.'

And it wasn't until after Peter Beardsley hit the bar and the roar of the crowd subsided, and with the Liverpool goalie still yelling at the police to open the gates of pens 3 and 4 which led onto the track, that a policeman ran onto the pitch and the game was finally stopped at 3.06.

As more Liverpool fans came over the perimeter fence and spilled onto the pitch, I could see some seemed to be dropping to the ground, while others were calling out for help or attempting resuscitation on those lying injured. But as I stood up and desperately scanned the ground, try as I might, I could not see my husband or my two precious girls and I thought, *This can't be true. This can't be happening. Not on such a lovely sunny April day.*

Chapter 11

Tragically, we later learned that due to serious policing and other failures outside the ground, a near-fatal crush had developed around the turnstiles at the Leppings Lanes end. To relieve the pressure, the match commander, Chief Superintendent David Duckenfield, had given the disastrous order to open exit gate C, without closing the tunnel that led to pens 3 and 4. This meant another two thousand unsuspecting supporters – including children – headed towards the one area inside the ground marked 'standing' – then straight through the tunnel down to the already overcrowded pens 3 and 4. And once they'd started on that course, there was no turning back, as the tunnel had a downward slope. Had the tunnel leading down to pens 3 and 4 been closed off, as it had the year before, this would have prevented the disaster from happening. The fans could have been guided to the side pens where there was room for them all.

To make matters even worse, the police did not open the narrow metal exit gates at the front of pens 3 and 4 that would have alleviated the huge number of people being crushed in that confined space. We later learned they'd refused to do so because they thought the fans were rioting. Rioting? People were fighting for their lives in there – while the first thing the match commander did was to put it down to a public order situation and call for the dogs. Not ambulances. Not first aid. But dogs. While people were fighting for their lives and dying. That appals me to my core.

Later, we would also learn that a fleet of forty-four ambulances from different districts were parked up outside the ground, with equipment that could have saved lives and more than eighty trained medical staff on board, but access was delayed because the police had reported fighting and crowd problems, as Duckenfield, the man in charge, 'froze'.*

By the time the perimeter gates in pens 3 and 4 were finally opened, it was too late for many people to get out. They had been in that fatal crush since 2.45 and had been finding it difficult since 2.30. With the added pressure of the further two thousand people coming into the pens, a crush barrier had broken and those behind the barrier and in front of it, including by the gate in pen 3, had been crushed. Although people also lost their lives in other areas of pens 3 and 4, this was where the majority of people died.

Sarah and Vicki, being seasoned football supporters, knew that if you stand behind a crush barrier and the people behind push into you, you can get hurt. When the girls had realised there were problems, they had moved to a position in front of a barrier. The only barrier that broke. Thankfully, I did not know about this at the time as I could not have coped with it, but later both Trevor and I had the heart-breaking task of hearing this in evidence at both

---

* Duckenfield admitted he froze under cross-examination by Paul Greaney QC at the manslaughter trial in Feb 2019.

inquests. The girls had obviously thought they'd moved to a safe place but because of the sheer numbers of people in those pens, nowhere was safe and once the barrier went like a house of cards it left a pile of bodies in its wake. I couldn't see the bodies heaped up from where I was sitting, but I could see even more supporters lying on the pitch who were injured and dying, and even now I can still see them in my nightmares – whether I am asleep or awake.

Amidst the chaos we were not at first given any information and I was about to go and look for the girls, but then came an announcement over the tannoy for all of us to stay where we were, and for some reason I did as I was told. But by now I was so desperate I kept asking this guy beside me, 'Can you see a girl with blond hair? Can you see a smaller girl with dark hair? Is that them there? Can you see them? Blond hair and dark.'

Over and over I heard myself repeat it, but neither of us could see Vicki or Sarah because they were lying unconscious on the pitch, and I was looking for them to be standing and moving around. After what seemed like an age, I saw an ambulance arriving on the pitch and more police. 'Thank God,' I said out loud. 'Help at last.' But instead of the police assisting the injured, they formed a line across the centre of the pitch, which I found out later was to prevent the Liverpool fans attacking the Forest supporters. But it was ridiculous, as by this time whichever way you looked you could see the fans were trying to give mouth-to-mouth, while others tore down the hoardings to use as stretchers for the injured. It was at this point that I saw the ambulance shut its doors and begin to drive slowly back round the ground. For some reason, I have no idea why, I watched it like a rabbit caught in the headlights as it came directly towards me, then veered off and drove past me and out of the exit. I didn't know until later that Trevor and Vicki were inside that ambulance. Nor did I know then that my other daughter, Sarah, was beneath my feet, lying dead in the Sheffield Wednesday gymnasium that was already being used as a temporary mortuary.

It must have been about four o'clock when the Liverpool manager Kenny Dalglish made an announcement over the tannoy for everyone to keep calm, and the fans listened to Kenny because they respected him. I was now beyond desperate to search for Trevor and my girls, but we were still advised not to leave our seats. Every person in that ground had no choice but to stay and watch as fans, some of them doctors, tried to keep people alive. In retrospect, I should have forced my way onto that pitch to look for my family and I think too that I should have done something to help the injured fans lying there. However, at the time I didn't want to make things worse by not doing as I was told.

Eventually an announcement was made that the match had been abandoned and we could now leave the ground. The match? That was the last thing on my mind, and I made my way towards the rendezvous point at the little tobacconist shop outside the stadium, fully hoping to see my family there, but my heart sank when I saw the doorway was empty. As I stood waiting for them there, I watched the fans coming out of the Leppings Lane terrace. At first there was a mass of supporters streaming out, and I was scanning the crowd, hoping to see the girls and Trevor. They didn't come out.

But there were police officers standing around the exit there, and some of the fans started shouting at them, 'You bastards! F★★★ing murderers! People have died in there!'

That really frightened me again, and I tried not to listen to them.

Not long after, the crowds of supporters coming out began to thin but still there was no sign of Sarah and Vicki or Trevor. No matter how much I strained my eyes, I couldn't see them. They were the only people I needed to see. To know they were OK. I kept asking myself, *Where are they? Where have they gone?* As much as I didn't want to accept it, I knew then there was something wrong. Something must have happened to my family. I waited there until I was certain there was no one else left to come out of the Leppings Lanes exit.

A male and a female police officer were standing close by, to my left. I went up to them and explained the situation: 'My husband and two daughters were on the Leppings Lane terraces this afternoon. I've got no money, no car keys, I'm in a strange city. Can you help me, please?'

'Oh,' they replied nonchalantly, 'they're setting up a "help place" at the back of the North Stand. If you go there, they might be able to help.'

Looking back, I can't explain why I did exactly as I was told and didn't even query it. Perhaps it was because I was still trying to protect myself, or maybe it was because I had always respected the police and trusted them to do the right thing. So, I went back round to the North Stand where I had just come from. Along the side of the wall adjacent to the North Stand was the footballers' gymnasium.

Outside the main doors to it, a trestle table had been set out where several police officers were standing with clipboards and lists. There were a lot of people, I couldn't count how many, queuing up to speak to the officers about their missing relatives and friends. Although people were obviously confused and distraught, the police were moving them on very quickly. When it came to my turn, I said again, 'I'm looking for my daughters and my husband. They were on the Leppings Lane terraces and they still haven't come out. Can you help me? I need help, please. I am in a strange city, I have no money, no car keys and I don't know what to do next.'

One of officers replied casually, 'Oh, go back to the car, love. They'll have gone back to the car.'

I was astounded by his attitude and that pejorative use of the word 'love' and told him, 'There is absolutely no way my husband and daughters would have come off that terrace and left me standing in a shop doorway, knowing that I would have just witnessed this disaster and knowing that I'd have no idea if they were OK or not. What you are telling me to do doesn't make sense.'

'I'm sorry, love,' he replied. 'That is all I can say to you, we've got no girls here.'

At the time I didn't take in what he meant about having no girls there. He was referring to my daughters as if they were little girls, when he hadn't even asked me how old they were. But once again, I did exactly as I was told – even though it was illogical – and walked back to the car.

Along the way I saw a man and woman coming towards me. 'Are you OK?' they called.

'I'm looking for my husband and daughters,' I shouted back. 'They were on the Leppings Lane terraces!'

The couple exchanged a concerned glance with each other, and replied that they hoped I would find them, and kept on walking.

As I turned into the enormous car park by the ground, I could see our silver car glinting in the late afternoon sunshine. It was the only car left in this entire car park – but still there was no sign of Sarah and Vicki, or Trevor. But I kept on walking to the car, even though I knew I couldn't open it, and I stood by the car door waiting.

I must have stood there for another ten minutes or more, when a police car pulled into the deserted car park and drove straight up to me. The policeman wound down his window and said, 'Get in the back of the car.' It was so strange: there was no introduction and no word of explanation, and even as I told him about trying to find my husband and daughters, that was all he said. I assumed the couple who'd spoken to me had flagged him down and told him about me.

The officer then drove me down to the Hamilton Road police station in Sheffield, which they had set up as HQ for the disaster – though no one told me this at the time. The officer dropped me off there and said, 'Go inside and tell them what you've told me.'

And then he was gone. So, I went in and told the police officer at the counter who I was looking for and that they had been in the disaster. And then I told him again. In fact, I don't know how many times I repeated myself: 'I'm looking for my two daughters and my husband. They were on the Leppings Lane terraces.'

And like all the other officers, he replied, 'OK, love.'

Love. How I hate the misuse of that word now. It was so patronising, so insensitive. Eventually he took me into a small room where another man was waiting who looked every bit as frightened as I was feeling. All the police officer said was, 'Wait in here, love.' So, I sat down and neither myself nor this poor man spoke; we sat there in silence and shock. Then the door opened, and a man in a dog collar popped his head round and I thought, *Oh my God, he's come to tell us they are dead!*

But all this poor vicar had done was open the wrong door. It was then that the chap sitting beside me and I first spoke. I said, 'I thought that was going to be bad news.' And he replied, 'So did I.' And that was when he told me, 'I'm looking for my eighteen-year-old son who was on the Leppings Lane terraces.'

And I said, 'I'm looking for my daughters and husband who were also on there.'

We spoke for a while about our missing relatives and how frightened we were, then the police came and took us to a boys' club across the road, which they said was being set up as a centre for people like us, who were looking for friends and relatives who had been at the match. The hall was musty and I felt as if we were in a scene from an old wartime film, where the vicar arrives, chairs are put out and an officious-looking person bustles around with a clipboard trying to sort things out, while a policeman stands by on duty. And this poor man and I were sitting there, watching all this going on, when all we really wanted to know was what had happened to our children. Where were they? How were they? When could we take them home? But the police were telling us absolutely nothing. We were expected to sit there and wait, which we did for over an hour, and then a trolley with a tea urn and cups and saucers on it was wheeled in. I didn't get a cup of tea, though – not that I could have drunk it – because another police officer arrived at this point and came over to me.

'We need you back at the police station. We need descriptions of the people you are looking for.'

And back I was taken across the road and seated in an upstairs room opposite a male and female officer, where I began to describe Sarah, Vicki and Trevor in detail. But even so, they kept asking more questions: 'Did they have any moles?' 'Did they have any scars?' 'Did they have any credit cards on them?' I was desperately trying to be helpful, and to get it right because I wanted them to find the girls. 'Did they have any distinctive marks?' 'Did they have tattoos?' 'What were they wearing?' Hair colour, eye colour, height. Everything. Right down to intimate details of what their naked bodies were like, which should have set off the alarm bells – but it didn't because I still had hope and didn't believe the worst because I didn't want to.

At this point, I still didn't know what had happened, as the police were saying nothing about the disaster and they gave us no information at all. The questioning took a long time, until finally, I was taken back to the boys' club and told to wait there again. By this time there were a few more people in there, looking for their loved ones, and gradually the hall began to fill up.

It was about a quarter to seven by now, two hours since I was meant to have met Trevor and my girls in the tobacconist's doorway. Unable to sit down any longer, I began pacing around the hall while I waited for news of my family. A Catholic priest then arrived with a man in his early thirties, who I couldn't help noticing had a lady's handbag over his arm. The priest came over and asked me, 'Can I be of any assistance?' I repeated yet again that I was looking for my two daughters and my husband. 'I can't find them anywhere,' I told him over and over. Then he gestured to the man with the handbag. 'This man,' he said, 'has lost his wife.' I looked at the man and I said, 'Oh, sorry, I hope you find her.' The man just stared back at me open-mouthed as the priest said, 'Oh no, she's dead. She died.'

At which point I thought, *What? What the hell's going on here? I have to get out of this place.*

Chapter 12

Although I had no cash or credit cards on me, and had no idea what I was going to do to find my family, I knew I couldn't just stay there in the hall and do nothing, so I made for the door. But as I did so, I bumped into a man on his way in. I think he could see I was how distressed I was, and he stopped and introduced himself to me. His name was Alan Dunkley, a social worker, and he asked me the same question as everyone else had, 'Are you OK?'

'I'm looking for my husband and my daughters, so no. No, I'm not OK!' I replied.

Alan offered to drive me to the Northern General Hospital in Sheffield to see if they were there. This was my first real positive offer of help, and a massive wave of relief swept over me.

On the way to the hospital, I asked Alan if he wouldn't mind going via the football ground,

'I want to make sure Trevor and the girls aren't looking for me there,' I told him.

Alan agreed and as we drove slowly past the Hillsborough Stadium, I could just make out the North Stand, where I thought I saw Sarah standing in the street by the side of the ground.

I asked Alan to stop the car: 'I think I saw Sarah down there!' Alan immediately pulled up and looked where I was pointing, and said, 'No, there's no one there.'

'I must have been mistaken,' I told him, though later I would learn that where I thought I had seen her was the gymnasium, which was being used as a temporary mortuary. That was exactly where Sarah had been when I'd asked for help from the police officer a few hours earlier. She had been carried in there at half past four that afternoon on one of the sheets of tin hoarding that fans were using as stretchers. I am sure now that Sarah had been trying to guide me to her. How I wish now I had gone down there, pushed past the officers and found Sarah in there.

We carried on to the Northern General Hospital and Alan came in with me to help me look for the girls. I'm thankful that from that point onwards I wasn't alone.

We went up to reception and I asked, 'Do you have a Sarah or Victoria Hicks here? Or a Trevor Hicks?'

'We've had a Victoria here,' the receptionist replied.

We've had *a Victoria?* I repeated her words in my head, and went over to Alan. 'That must mean Vicki's been here, they've treated her, and she's gone. Vicki's OK!' I was so relieved.

Then I saw a nurse coming over to me. 'Are you Mrs Hicks?' she asked. I nodded, 'Then would you mind coming with me?'

Alan said he'd wait for me if I wanted to speak to her alone, but I was far too upset for that.

'No, please don't leave me on my own. I don't want to be on my own again,' I told him.

We were then taken into a small treatment room with a bed in the corner and equipment on the side. The nurse went to close the door behind her, and I panicked, 'No, don't close the door!' For some reason, I didn't want to be shut in this room. The next thing I was aware of was a doctor, standing in the doorway. He was only young, and he couldn't bring himself to look at me. He was carrying a clipboard and asked me, 'Are you the mother of Victoria Jane Hicks?' Then he started to describe her. I looked at Alan and I looked back at the doctor, who never once looked up from this clipboard but read from it like a script. I knew what he was going to say. He was going to tell me that Vicki was dead, and there was no way I could allow him to tell me that – I wouldn't have been able to take it. So, to stop him saying those words, I said to him, 'You're going to tell me Vicki's dead, aren't you?' And he finally looked up, and he replied, 'Yes.'

As I started to walk out of the room I noticed a vicar, who began saying all kinds of religious stuff to me. I told him not to come anywhere near me, and not to tell me how good God is, as I brushed past him and left the room. I candidly told him what he could do with his God.

As we walked down the corridor outside the room, I approached a member of the hospital staff.

'I would like to see Vicki,' I told her. 'I'm her mum.'

She had to go and take advice, but when she came back, she replied, 'No, I'm sorry, I'm afraid you can't do that. She is nothing to do with you now, she is the property of the coroner of South Yorkshire.'

I was stunned; I couldn't believe what they were saying to me – it made no sense. The next thing I knew, a nurse was handing me a polythene bag and an envelope. She told me they were Vicki's things, but I was too stunned to look inside. I simply could not comprehend any of what was happening. I had gone out to a game of football with Vicki and was going home with a white plastic bag, and a large brown envelope instead. I was standing there when a nurse came over and informed me, 'Your husband Trevor was here with Vicki, but he has now gone to the Hallamshire Hospital to look for your other daughter, who wasn't brought here.'

I turned to Alan. 'At least I'm not being told she's dead yet,' I said, hoping and praying that Sarah was still alive.

Then the nurse came back shortly after and said, 'We've telephoned the Hallamshire and your husband is on his way back here. He's got a young woman with him.'

My heart skipped a beat. I was so distraught about Vicki, but Sarah was alive! I said to Alan, 'I'm going to have to pull myself together, because Sarah is going to be very upset about Vicki.'

My thoughts were all with my eldest daughter now and how I was going to break this terrible news to her, and how I could help her through this appalling tragedy of losing her little sister. As we waited outside by the entrance to the hospital, I said to Alan who, being a social worker would know about these things, 'You're going to have to help me with Sarah, please.' He said he would do whatever he could.

Then I saw Trevor arrive and walk up the path towards us with a young woman beside him – but I could see it wasn't Sarah. It was explained to me that she was another social worker who'd been assigned to help Trevor at the Hallamshire because they worried that in his search for Sarah, he'd had to look at other deceased people who'd come in

CHAPTER 12

that night. The social worker had brought Trevor back here again because our car was still in the car park next to the football ground – and here I was, believing I was about to be reunited with my daughter. I cannot describe how I felt. I screamed across the path at Trevor, 'Where is she? Where's Sarah?'

When Trevor got close enough, he said to me, 'Jenni, when I left Sarah on the pitch, she was in a worse state than Vicki.'

I said to him, 'Oh please God, not both of them! Not both of them, please!'

He told me that as the horror had unravelled at the match, he'd searched for the girls and found them, as if by some miracle, lying side by side on the pitch by the goal. With no medical facilities, he'd tried to revive them himself and in the midst of all the chaos around them, he'd shouted for help. Another Liverpool supporter, a doctor, had rushed over to try to revive Sarah while Trevor tried to clear Vicki's airways by sucking vomit from her mouth. When the ambulance had arrived on the pitch, a young PC and a Liverpool supporter had helped him to carry Vicki and put her in. But in the few seconds that it had taken him to rush back to Sarah to carry her to the ambulance, it was already full. He'd then been faced with the most agonising dilemma of whether to go to the hospital with Vicki or to stay with Sarah. Believing that Sarah would follow behind in the next ambulance, he had left her on the pitch, not realising that no more ambulances would be coming through. For Trevor to have had to make the decision to leave Sarah there must have been torture. Of the seven females who died at Hillsborough, Vicki was the only one who made it to hospital.

At the hospital, Trevor asked me if I'd been in to see Vicki.

'I wanted to,' I told him, 'but they wouldn't let me.'

He explained that the doctors had tried for twenty minutes to resuscitate Vicki before they gave up.

'Then they changed her into a gown, and she is now in a side room in the chapel of rest,' he said.

I really couldn't take this in, not at all.

'My wife would like to see our daughter!' Trevor shouted the nurse over. 'I can take her. I know which room she's in.'

'No, sorry, you can't do that!' the nurse replied.

Trevor looked stunned. 'Why on earth not?'

'You can't see her,' she said. 'You're not allowed.'

Not allowed? So, we had brought a child into the world, raised her, and now she's dead we're not allowed to see her? I couldn't take it in, but I had never seen Trevor so angry.

'I'm sorry, but my wife wants to see our daughter,' he said, 'and if you are not going to allow us to see her, then I'm afraid I'm going to go straight past you and take my wife in to see her! Nobody is going to stop us!'

The nurse immediately brought a police officer over as back-up.

'I'm afraid you can't see your daughter,' he said. 'You're not allowed to, because she is now the property of the coroner of South Yorkshire.'

'The property of the coroner?' Trevor repeated.

'Yes, she is absolutely nothing to do with you two any more,' he continued. 'And in any case, she's not here now, we've taken her back to the football ground. The coroner ordered it so that all the dead could be together.'

I was just zombie-like at this point. Alan offered to drive us back to the football ground along with Hilary, the other social worker who was with Trevor. As we left the hospital, the sun had gone down. It was cold, dark and we still didn't know if Sarah was alive or dead.

Back at the ground, we walked round to the entrance, where there was a police sergeant on duty with another officer. Trevor told him who we were and why we were there, and he bluntly replied, 'You're not allowed in.'

We looked at each other in shock, then the sergeant continued, 'We're not ready for you yet. We haven't got it set up properly. You can't come in. Anyway, they all need to have post-mortems. Now go away and come back later.'

I was shocked. I didn't even know that my eldest daughter was dead. I blurted out, 'I don't want them to have post-mortems! They haven't even had any operations or got any scars on them!'

The policeman shrugged, 'You've got no choice, love.'

There it was, that 'love' again. They said it so many times to me that night. He went on to describe what the exemptions were for post-mortems.

Trevor, who had always been respectful of police officers and authority, just looked at this copper and, white with anger, went to take a swing at him.

'If you don't let us in, I'm going to knock you out! We are coming in, no matter what!' he yelled at him.

Alan stepped in and he and Hilary tried to settle Trevor down. Then Trevor said to the officer, 'This is what I am going to do now: I am taking my wife back to the car

93

park and then we are going to collect our car and come back here again. It will only take ten minutes, and then we are going to come in and neither you nor anyone else is going to stop us.'

Then, looking the sergeant straight in the eye, he said, 'Do you get that? Because that is what is going to happen. Trust me!'

We got back in Alan's car and went to the car park, where Trevor and I got in our car, and Hilary and Alan followed us back to the ground. When we got there, there were two burly officers in leather jackets waiting for us. Tough-looking guys, they introduced themselves as belonging to the Criminal Investigation Department (CID). I was anxious that they were going to tell us the same as the sergeant, so it really surprised us when they said, 'Come along, we're going to take you in.'

The four of us went into the ground with the CID officers, where we were taken inside the gymnasium and shown a large green baize board with dozens of tiny polaroid photographs of the dead pinned on it. A police officer was standing at the side of the board.

'Right, can you look at the photographs and identify your daughters?' No please or pleasantries, nothing.

Trevor said, 'I have already identified Vicki at the hospital.'

The officer replied, 'I want you to look again and identify her from these photographs as well.'

So, we had to look at all the rows and rows of photographs of dead people. Of people's faces in their body bags, who only hours earlier had been living and breathing. It felt like I was intruding on every person's privacy. It was

94

impossible to describe how I felt, yet with every picture I looked at, I also felt hope that if I couldn't see Sarah, she had survived. And we had to look very closely at the photographs, because the police didn't help by even filtering out the men from the women, or by ages, despite all the school children among them. Then I saw Vicki's beautiful little face looking out from the board. I shall never ever forget that moment. It will stay with me forever.

But I couldn't see Sarah's photo on the board, and once again I felt there was hope.

'Sarah's not there,' I told the police officer.

'Look again, love,' he replied.

That word 'love' again, with almost an impatience to it. So, I did look again, even harder this time, at all those poor people who had died in the crush. I realised that, because Vicki had been to the hospital, she had been cleaned up, so she had been easy to recognise. It was then I was able to make out Sarah among the Polaroids.

'Oh. There she is.'

I was trembling now. My mouth was dry and, in that heart-shattering moment, all my hope was gone. I realised I had lost both my girls and there could be no more denial. It was *the* very worst moment of my life. They had both gone and nothing would or ever could be the same again.

Chapter 13

I had just identified my girls in the photographs, and I was completely numb.

'Do you want to see them?' an officer asked us, bringing me round, and I thought, *I have been asking to see Vicki for the past two hours.*

'Yes,' I said.

'Together? Or separately?'

'Together,' I replied.

Here we were in the worst possible of situations, yet so far there'd been not one ounce of compassion in that place. Not one.

We were directed to stand behind a screen where two body bags were wheeled to us on small trolleys, very low to the ground. The two CID officers stood with us while another officer unzipped the bags. My heart was broken in pieces, but oddly I felt overwhelming relief at seeing my girls again and dropped to my knees on the floor. Vicki was on my left, Sarah on the right and I got down between the trolleys and I lifted Vicki up and I hugged her, and then I did the same with Sarah. The numbness that had started in the football ground had now become total. Vicki was ice cold and still wearing a white hospital gown, while Sarah was still in her clothes. I hugged Sarah and I could not believe it as she was still warm. Sarah was as warm as toast, completely the opposite to Vicki. I looked up and said to the police officers, 'Are you sure she is dead? Because she's really warm – can you get somebody to check if she is really dead?'

These two tough-looking CID officers in their leather jackets had tears streaming down their faces. They were the only ones who showed us any empathy at all. I always remember that, and I've always had this feeling – even now – that I should have insisted a doctor was brought in to see Sarah because she should not have been as warm as she was, especially as it was now after nine o'clock at night and she was only wearing a T-shirt and her 501s. She didn't wear socks and she didn't have her jacket on, which had come off in the mayhem, along with her brown DM shoes. So really Sarah should have felt cold to the touch, not warm and certainly not six hours after the disaster. I wished I had pursued it further, and I still do. But at least I did question it with the police.

As soon as I stood up, I watched as they were zipped up and wheeled away to another part of the gym. There are no words to describe how I felt. Trevor and I were led over to one side of the gym where there was a large wooden table. I was still clutching Vicki's bag of belongings when the police handed me Sarah's black Swatch watch, just like Vicki's, and her leather flying jacket.

Alan Dunkley later told me that, where we were sitting, behind us there were rows and rows of the dead in body bags laid out on the floor. Trevor and I were told to sit at one side of that table, while a policewoman and a policeman sat facing us as if we were about to be inter-rogated. Which I soon found we were, as they asked us a barrage of questions and got us to make statements about what had happened that day.

'What time did you leave home?' they asked. 'What did you have for breakfast?' 'Which route did you drive?'

I couldn't understand it. Surely, we should be the ones asking them the questions and *they* should have been giving us some answers. But we wanted to help them and so we answered honestly and truthfully. I didn't like the ques-tioning, so looked inside the brown envelope the nurse had given me at the hospital, containing Vicki's belong-ings. I opened and emptied it onto the table, and Vicki's black Swatch watch, her earrings and her signet ring fell out, which Sarah had given to Vicki when it no longer fitted her. I put the signet ring on my finger, and both of the girls' Swatch watches on the same wrist, and put the earrings back in the envelope. I desperately wanted to look in the bag of clothes the hospital had given me. To touch and smell the clothes that she had taken so long to choose to wear before we set off this morning. But I didn't.

'Did you have any alcohol?' 'Did you stop on the way for alcohol?' 'Did you have a bottle of wine with your lunch?' The questioner continued.

Everything was about alcohol. We had only just seen our daughters in body bags and that was all they were talking about. It must have been over an hour of questioning, and they got us to make statements which would later be used against Trevor, including the timings on it, down to the last second. The police must have known that they should never have taken those statements from us without us having a solicitor present, but we didn't know it then, and were too traumatised to even think about it. So they took advantage of the state we were in. Even when I asked to go to the ladies, a police officer escorted me and stayed there while I went to the loo and then escorted me back again as if I was a suspect. And then it was back to the interrogation all about alcohol again. My daughters were teenagers, one was still at school, so all this talk about alcohol didn't make sense to me at the time.

After midnight, when the questioning was finally over and we were free to leave, a doctor arrived at the gym and offered me a sedative. I really felt that I had slipped into a parallel universe by this time and that nothing was real, but I refused it. Looking back now, I often wish I'd said to him, 'Would you please go and have another look at Sarah, because she's still warm.'

But I didn't. Instead, I asked them if we could take Sarah and Vicki home with us. All I wanted was to put them in the car and bring them home.

The police offered to find us accommodation in Sheffield for the night, or a police driver to take us back to London, but I didn't want that. I wanted us to get back home as soon as we could, and once we got there, for everything to be normal again – though I knew my two daughters were now lying in body bags on a cold gymnasium floor. We'd gone to a football match as a family and driven home at night with an empty backseat. Who'd have thought *that* when we'd left home this morning? All I had now was

Vicki's signet ring on my finger, the girls' watches on my wrist, the plastic bag of Vicki's clothes and Sarah's leather jacket, which I cuddled to me as I returned home, no longer a mum.

Chapter 14

I don't remember much of that journey home. I thought I must have gone to sleep. Trevor drove us, and we didn't arrive back until after two in the morning. I couldn't wait to get out of the car and I rushed straight into the house and up the stairs to check if Sarah and Vicki were in their bedrooms. I know it doesn't make sense, but I wanted the day before to have been a bad dream. Of course, their beds were empty, which was a terrible reinforcement.

Trevor started closing all the curtains in the house. For some reason I couldn't bear that and threw them open, even though it was pitch-black and cold outside in the early hours of that April morning. As Trevor started making phone calls to tell his family what had happened, I went through our picnic bag, and took out the cheese and pickle sandwiches I'd made for Vicki for the journey home. They were her favourite, but Vicki wouldn't be needing them now, and I threw them in the bin. Or the mint Cornettos she'd put in the freezer to save for when we came back from the game. They went in the bin too.

I then took her jeans out of the white polythene bag they'd given me at the hospital. They had huge grass stains on them, and I thought, *Vicki will never wear them like this.* So I put them in the washing machine and they must have gone round several cycles, but still the stains of Hillsborough would not come out.

It was then that I thought of the flowers we had planted earlier that year, and in the next moment I was rifling through the kitchen drawers for a pair of scissors. I went out into the garden; it was still the middle of the night but with the outside light on I could see the tulips in full bloom that only last autumn Sarah and Vicki had planted around the edge of the front lawn and all the way down the side of the steps to the house. They'd embedded them in the soil in alternate colours: one red, one yellow, one red, one yellow and so on, which meant that when they came out, they'd be in the colours of the Liverpool strip as it was at that time. I began cutting the stems of these beautiful flowers. As I did so, I looked up and saw Trevor standing on the doorstep watching me. He was probably wondering what I was doing out there in the early hours of the morning. But I didn't stop until I had picked every single one. Then I went back in the house carrying an armful of the flowers. I put them into the large bowl-like vases we had and filled the living room and hall with the red and yellow tulips.

Trevor and I never went to bed that night. He was still wearing his jeans which, like Vicki's, had grass stains on them, though his were all down the front where he'd been kneeling over the girls on the pitch. I curled up in a ball on the sofa where I used to sprawl out with the girls and watch TV, but every time I dropped off to sleep, I suddenly woke with a start. I could feel my eyelids beginning to get heavy again when at around four in the morning the phone went. I had no notion of it being a strange time for someone to ring, but it was one of Sarah's friends from university, Linda. She sounded worried.

'There's something on the news,' she said, 'and I'm so sorry to ring you at this hour, but I can't sleep.'

'Don't worry about it,' I said, unable to think straight. 'I can't either.'

'Well, thank goodness you're all safely home,' Linda replied, exhaling with relief.

It was then I took a deep breath and, finally saying it out loud, I replied, 'No, Linda. Sarah and Vicki are dead.'

There was a silence at the other end of the phone, then she burst into floods of tears and the poor girl rang off.

The hours seemed to merge into one, and at around eight o'clock, while I was still on the sofa, the phone rang again. It was the mother of one of Vicki's friends, Nina, who also lived in Hatch End. Vicki and Nina were in the same form at Habs; they used to travel together on the school coach and spend time round each other's houses.

The voice at the other end of the phone said, 'I'm ringing because Nina is really concerned about Vicki. But I am so pleased to hear you're home.'

I guess people thought if there was a problem we would still be in Sheffield, but I couldn't grasp any of that now and replied, 'Well, Trevor and I are home, but Sarah and Vicki have both died.'

There was this pause again as there had been with Linda, and then she said, 'Do you want me to come over?'

'Yes, please,' I replied.

So, she came over, bringing Nina with her, and they started making tea. I started telling her about the grass stains on Vicki's jeans, which were really upsetting me.

'I can't get these grass stains out,' I said, 'and she won't wear them again if they're stained. Can you help me get the stains out?' And I kept repeating it to her. 'Can you help me get these stains out, please?'

She gently took them from me and said, 'We'll try something that will help to get them out, Jenni, don't worry.'

'And there's this too,' I said, producing a white T-shirt with a large gold logo on it from the plastic bag. But the T-shirt was also covered in the grass stains, and again only on the back where Vicki had been laid on the pitch.

'I need to put this in a really hot wash to get it clean,' I said, 'but if I do, it will shrink, and I don't want to ruin Vicki's clothes for her. You know how she loves her clothes.'

'We'll find something,' Nina's mum said calmly, not making me feel silly for how I was behaving.

Looking back, she seemed to understand where I was at in my head, and that it wouldn't be a good idea to say, 'It doesn't really matter now, does it?' because to me it really did. She took the T-shirt and, as with the jeans, quietly tucked them away out of sight and went to the kitchen and started making tea. I followed her in and sat in an almost trance-like state on a stool at the end of the island unit. Trevor and I still hadn't had anything to eat, but neither of us could think about that.

'At least have a biscuit, try a biscuit,' Nina's mum tried to coax us, but I couldn't. The very idea of it made me feel sick.

From the moment Nina and her mum had arrived that morning, until they went home late that night, they seemed to do just what was needed. It was a kind of security having them there because we had no family with us at that point; they were all up in the north-east. Trevor had phoned to let them know, and they were making arrangements to come down that night. Everything felt so unreal at this point, I was just waiting for things to get back to normal. However, we soon learned that a list of people who had died at Hillsborough had been put up on Ceefax* at midday, including their ages and where they came from. With both the BBC and ITV headquarters being so close to us in central London, reporters and cameramen were at our door within an hour or so of this going live.

---

* The first teletext information service. It was on the BBC.

Chapter 15

We lived at the last house in a small close. There was one road in and out, with a farm and a field with horses opposite the house, and a golf course to the side. It really was a perfect place for children to play because it was a dead end with no through traffic. But now the press and camera crews were all parked up on one side of the road, and they started taking it in turns to walk down the steps to our front door and knock on it, always keeping the cameras rolling in case they caught a glimpse of me or Trevor opening the door. By this time the phone had started ringing; no sooner would we put the phone down than it would start again. It never stopped over the next few days. It was relentless.

We were ex-directory, but still they'd managed to get hold of our phone number. They were continually knocking on the door as well. We were under siege, and yet here we were, still dressed as we had been when we left home at ten the morning before. No hair combed. No shower. We still hadn't been to bed, and now this.

In the end, Trevor rang the Press Association and complained. They advised him: 'As long as they are not on your property but stay outside on the pavement or the road, they are not legally doing anything wrong. So, my advice to you is to give them a press conference. Find a couple of photographs, one of Sarah one of Vicki, and go out and make an announcement, just say "OK, I am going to say this once, and only once."'

The journalists all gathered like locusts around Trevor as he did exactly as the Press Association had advised. He'd asked me beforehand which pictures to give them, so I chose the two that I knew the girls liked and watched from the window as the press sellotaped the girls' pictures to the side of one of their vans and photographed them, a myriad of flashes going off. The media still use those pictures of Sarah and Vicki, even today.

On the Sunday evening, Trevor's mum and family arrived from the north-east. The next morning Trevor's sister June looked at me and said, 'I think it might be a good idea if you tried to have a shower and put some clean clothes on, Jenni. It might make you feel a bit better.' We hadn't taken off our clothes or had a shower for at least two days.

But I couldn't take my clothes off. I felt as if they were stopping me from falling apart. They were the only thing holding me together.

'You will probably feel better,' June persisted.

Then Trevor stepped in, 'Yes, come on, Jenni, we both might feel better if we shower,' he said, and lightly took my arm.

'I'll only do it if you stand in the bathroom with me while I get in the shower,' I said. I just needed somebody to be there.

Trevor nodded and did as I asked, but after I'd showered and washed my hair, I didn't feel any better. In the hours after the game was called off, my clothes felt as if they'd become my only protection. If it hadn't been suggested to me to change them, I would have kept them on for God knows how long. What did clothes matter now? What did anything matter, least of all the everyday act of washing and dressing myself, which each morning after this became an enormous mountain to climb. From a fifteen-minute job before I got the girls off to school, it had suddenly become a huge effort.

Trevor had his own struggles too. When Nina and her mum left that first day, he busied himself making tea for his family and our various visitors. I remember his brother-in-law asking him, 'How on earth did you drive back home from Sheffield after that?'

And I piped up, 'Yes, and I was no help at all! I fell asleep.'

'No, you didn't,' Trevor said. 'You talked to me all the way home from Sheffield, you kept me going. And you kept me from turning around and looking for the girls in the back of the car.'

I had no memory of any of that, though I recalled constantly checking to see if Sarah and Vicki were sitting in the back myself, and thinking, *Where are they? Where have they got to?*

I thought I'd been no help to Trevor at all and this kind of memory loss was something I would later seek help with.

Even though Trevor had given his 'press conference', it made no difference. The journalists still hounded us. My mother-in-law went out to fetch the milk off the doorstep and, because they were unable get me and Trevor, they filmed her instead. It was crazy, and clearly there were few lengths they wouldn't go to. On the Monday, which should have been Vicki's first day back at school, shockingly, a TV film crew went up to Haberdashers' school and somehow managed to slip into Vicki's classroom and film her empty desk. The teacher hadn't arrived yet, but Vicki's friends and form mates were sitting there and obviously the TV company, with no thought for Vicki's classmates or the family, thought it would make a good story. A close friend of Vicki's then arrived and asked her classmates, 'What are they doing here? Why are they filming Vicki's desk?' One of the girls told her, 'Vicki has died.' Her friend was horrified, 'Vicki is dead?' She couldn't believe it. 'She died on Saturday, at the football match,' another girl told her. This was too much for Vicki's friend, who collapsed and had to be rushed to hospital where they found she'd gone into kidney failure, possibly due to the shock.

The school's head teacher decided to make an announcement in assembly so that all the school got to know about it, rather than let news of Vicki go round as rumour. The head also spoke to the film crew and told them they could not use anything they'd shot as they didn't have permission to be in the school in the first place. But to prevent the film crew from harassing Vicki's distressed classmates outside the gates, she offered to do an interview with the TV company. They were happy with that, so she talked about what a very bright pupil and vivacious girl Vicki was, who'd had a great future ahead of her, and she spoke highly of her sister Sarah being a pupil there too, and how sad the school was to have lost them both. It was so kind of her to do the interview. I was comforted by her words, and the words of those who'd come to our house to offer their condolences.

The minister from the Baptist church also came to the house to offer comfort. I told him about the conversation I'd had with Sarah two weeks earlier, before that fateful day, and how she'd said she was going to die before me. I also told him how guilty I now felt at not pushing her more about why she felt that way. I should have asked her, 'Are you unhappy, Sarah? Is there something you are not telling me?'

The minister spoke about the 'premonition', as he called it, at the funeral service. But it wasn't a premonition, because if Sarah had for one moment thought she was going to die at the football match, she wouldn't have gone or let us go either, and she certainly wouldn't have taken Vicki in that Leppings Lane terrace with her. To my mind, Sarah just had this feeling that, whenever the end of her life came, it would be before mine, and she was telling me what she wanted at her funeral. But of course, the 'premonition' would soon be a big story in some sectors of the popular press. Though this story would pale into insignificance compared with the one that was about to break, and which would come to symbolise the struggle for truth and justice for my daughters and the other victims that still continues some thirty-two years later, as indeed it would for all those who lost children, parents, partners and friends as a result of that day.

Chapter 16

In the early days after losing the girls, we weren't walking alone. Our friends Chris and Jeff would come over to our house every morning. They had known the girls for years, and they both took two weeks off work to spend every day with me and Trevor. But I was so taken up with my own grief, it wasn't until later that I realised they were in shock about it all too. 'I have never seen anybody as close as you three were,' Chris said to me one day, and we were, but I could see the sadness in Chris's eyes as she said this.

Trevor's family had gone home on Monday morning, and Jeff carried on fielding calls from the press. He became our receptionist for the next two weeks, while Chris helped with the basics of day-to-day living. As the days went by, Trevor and I realised we wanted answers to our questions, but so far nothing had been forthcoming from the police. But then we were visited by two family liaison officers, Graham McCombie and Julie Appleton, from the West Midlands Police. They told us they'd been assigned to work with several families who'd lost loved ones in the disaster and they were part of the investigation into the South Yorkshire Police (SYP). Through my grief and shock, I welcomed that.

On Graham and Julie's first visit to us, they brought Sarah's clothes with them: her 501s, belt, white T-shirt and one brown DM shoe (they couldn't find both). But because we were so distressed, neither had the heart to tell us this, and it would take several more trips before Graham could bring himself to get Sarah's clothes out of his car and hand them over to us. However, aside from them telling us there was going to be an inquiry into the disaster, most of what we knew came from the press. Trevor would go down to the village to fetch up all the newspapers each morning and return with a great pile of them, running the gauntlet with the press camped outside. I could see the irony of that, even then.

It was just four days after the disaster that Trevor came back ashen-faced. 'Perhaps you shouldn't read that,' he said, as I took the top one from the pile and saw blazoned across the front page of the *Sun* in inverted commas, 'The Truth'. As we read the article, our mouths fell open. The article claimed that the Liverpool fans were drunk, they'd urinated on the dead, picked their pockets and robbed them. They'd arrived late without tickets and tried to push their way in, forcing open exit gate C. They'd spat at the police and tried to hamper their rescue efforts. They also reported that, 'In one shameful episode a gang of Liverpool fans noticed that the T-shirt of a girl trampled to death had risen above her breasts. As a policeman struggled in vain to revive her, the mob jeered: "Throw her up here and we will f★★★ her."'

The article went on to say they thought the girl was the youngest of the Hicks sisters. They can only have got this detail from the South Yorkshire Police. I was stunned and I felt sick. How had they heard this over the crowd when they couldn't hear the fans' cries for help?

'They're lying,' I gasped, looking at Trevor, who was seething.

After the total shock at reading all these scurrilous claims and hurtful lies, it became quite obvious to us that they were trying to shift the blame onto the fans by suggesting they had killed their own. The whole article was a work of fiction. If it hadn't been for the fans doing whatever they could to help the injured, there'd have been far more than ninety-six fatalities. A hell of a lot more! Many fans had been heroic.

It just didn't match up with what I had seen. From where I'd been sitting, it had been clear from early on that there were problems with the filtering system of supporters as the side terraces were almost empty, while the central pens kept on filling up. I had been at the ground since 2 p.m. and not seen any drunken fans either. Of course, we didn't know then that the story was being fed by the police to White's Press Agency in Sheffield, though all the talk about alcohol when the police interviewed us in the temporary mortuary began to click into place. Trevor was bringing home copies of every newspaper and I could feel my heart sinking as I went through them and wondered what I would read next. They were all running similar stories, though using more cushioned terms to blame and stigmatise the Liverpool fans. The *Express* ran the headline, 'Police accuse drunken fans', while according to the *Sheffield Star*, 'Many supporters were still propping up bars at 2.30 p.m. They raced to the stadium arriving at the Leppings Lane end at the height of the crush. Some of them were the worse for drink, others without tickets were hoping to sneak in.' Hubble bubble toil and trouble . . . drunkenness and ticketlessness were now added to the equation.

They were described as 'beasts' by no less than Jacques Georges, President of UEFA, and as 'yobs' by John Williams of the *Liverpool Daily Post*. Radio and TV reports were also damning of the fans. Even Nottingham Forest Manager Brian Clough, who was at the Hillsborough game, blamed the fans, reiterating this in his autobiography and on a television chat show a few years later. I felt betrayed by the footballer my uncles and I had so admired while I was growing up.

We would soon realise that this was just the start of the rot – the covering up of the truth to protect the police. I had lost my innocent children and was having to read these vile and disgusting smears against them. And these smears, which would be perpetuated in other sectors of the media, would help to colour the public's perceptions of the fans, obstruct the victims' families from getting at the truth and pervert the course of justice for decades to come – which of course they were intended to do. I would not have believed this kind of thing existed before. How naive was I?

It was strange really, because with the girls going to a top independent school, Trevor being a managing director and us coming from London and travelling up as a family to the Liverpool games each week, we didn't fit into the narrative that the South Yorkshire Police and the press had concocted about the supporters. They must have resented that. On the other hand, at a local level, the media were fascinated by us, and when the *News at Ten* team came to our house to interview me and Trevor, they were always respectful. In fact, we got to know them so well they would send us a card at Christmas.

★

Since the girls died, I was having trouble eating properly. In those first weeks I survived on bananas, chocolate and Weetabix. I'd always been a chocoholic, but I started eating far too many chocolate bars. Cadbury's Caramel became my favourite, but despite that I was still losing weight. I also hadn't been able to sit down to eat at the table since the girls had gone, or to eat anything I would need a knife and fork for, and I especially couldn't eat the food that Vicki and Sarah loved best, because I would feel guilty that I was still able to eat all their favourites, while they no longer could. I suppose on one level it was survivor's guilt, but on another it was about my grief and yearning for the girls and our old lives together, cooking their favourites for them and us sitting round the table each evening talking and eating together. So, I just ate chocolate bars instead.

Even though I was struggling to look after myself, we experienced a great deal of kindness from strangers. Within days of the tragedy, our young postman stopped putting our post through the letterbox and began knocking on the door with great big grey sacks full of mail for us every day. People sent flowers and letters to us from every corner of the world, often with nothing more written on the envelope than 'To Sarah and Vicki's Mum and Dad, London'. Those letters were people sharing their own stories with us, and their support helped to keep me and Trevor afloat. I would often sit and read the letters when I couldn't sleep at night, and there were so many flowers that every room in the house was filled with them. My friend Chris had to borrow vases from all the local florists to put them in.

All these were huge acts of kindness for which I will be forever thankful. I remember the Monday after the tragedy, lifting up the phone and a male voice introducing himself as Jimmy Tarbuck. He offered his condolences and asked if there was anything he could do to help. I remember calling out to Trevor to come and take the phone, because there was some bloke pretending to be Jimmy Tarbuck. But it really was him. So my apologies to Jimmy, if he heard what I said to Trevor. And there were others from within the world of football: we had a telephone call from David Dein, the vice chairman of Arsenal football club. I didn't know at the time, but his daughter attended the same school as Sarah and Vicki. He wanted to express his condolences and support, and asked permission to come and see us. He did, and his support continues to this day.

We were seeing the best of humanity from ordinary people, and sadly, from the police and those in power, the very worst.

Chapter 17

It was time to arrange the funerals. I remembered a conversation Sarah and I had had a couple of weeks before the match. She had been sitting at the kitchen island drinking coffee when she said matter-of-factly, 'Mum, when I finish at uni, I'm going to stay on in Liverpool.'

I looked at her a moment, but I wasn't surprised. I knew she loved it up there: the uni, the city and then of course Anfield. But with us being so tight-knit, it was going to be a wrench for me, and her sister too.

'Well, OK, I appreciate you telling me,' I replied. 'But you haven't been up there a year yet. Why don't you make that decision a bit nearer the time?'

'No, Mum,' she said in her gentle but determined way. 'I'm going to find a place and live there permanently one day.'

Of course, she was going to fly the nest one day, I told myself; she was a young woman – even though a part of me still saw Sarah and Vicki as my little girls.

But now, just a few weeks later, we were having to bury her. I started to think, how can I bring her back to London to have her buried here when she recently told me she wanted to stay in Liverpool?

Trevor was making all the funeral arrangements in Pinner with an undertaker who had been in the business for years.

When the elderly owner came over to make all the arrangements, he couldn't look at me without crying. Every time we met, out came the hanky and he would be really sobbing. On this particular day, he asked Trevor if they could go into the kitchen and talk because he couldn't be in the same room as me without crying. While they went off to discuss it, I mulled over what Sarah had said to me. And it struck me that, of course, she would want to be buried in Liverpool. Then I thought, *Well, I'm not splitting the girls up.* Besides, I knew Vicki was always telling her friends at Haberdashers' that Liverpool was the best place in the country, so she would be happy to be buried there too. But Trevor didn't know any of this. It was all just conversations going on in my head, and we were both so obviously grief-stricken that nothing really was normal.

Waking early one day from the little sleep I managed to have, I said to Trevor, 'You better get up, because we're going to Liverpool.'

He looked at me, bewildered. 'What are we going to Liverpool for?'

'To arrange to have the girls buried there.'

'But I've just arranged to have them buried here.'

I replied, 'Well, you can unarrange it.'

'Jenni, let me remind you, we are not from Liverpool,' he said. 'It won't be as easy as that. And where in Liverpool are you thinking of having them buried anyway?'

Although I didn't know the name of it yet, I already knew exactly where I wanted them buried. I had seen this lovely place we used to go past when we picked Sarah up from her halls of residence on our way to Anfield every other Saturday. There was a very beautiful tree-lined road, which we used to pass by, and Vicki would always say, 'I love it round here. It's gorgeous.'

With my mind resolved and feeling especially determined, I said to Trevor, 'Come on, I'll show you.'

Trevor, who was trying to be kind to me because I was so upset, got the car out and drove us to Liverpool. Almost three hours later, when we got to the cemetery, we went in and found the cemetery manager. We told him who we were, and I said, 'We would just like our girls to be buried here, please.'

He looked at us a moment and then he went towards his van. 'Get in your car and follow me,' he said. 'I know exactly where the girls can go.' And it was as easy as that.

Trevor said, 'You do know that we're from London? We don't live here.'

But this kind man showed us a lovely spot, under a majestic, tall evergreen monkey puzzle tree, and he said, 'This will be perfect for your girls, they would love the tree.'

I don't know how he knew that, but he was right – they would absolutely love it.

He asked us the name of our undertakers in London, and then he said, 'OK, leave the rest to me.'

So we didn't have to make any other arrangements. I couldn't believe something so complicated was made so easy by this lovely stranger, the complete antithesis of what had happened at Hillsborough only a few days earlier and which had brought us here. The cemetery manager contacted one of the local firms used by other families of the Liverpool fans who had died, and he also contacted our undertakers in

London, and between them they worked together. They were amazing, really amazing. I can never thank them enough.

As we were driving out of the cemetery, we heard on the local radio that LFC had opened up Anfield for people to go and pay their respects. We decided we'd like to go to Anfield too, and so went into a local florist and bought some flowers to put on the Kop, in the place where Sarah and Vicki had stood to watch Liverpool play. We knew our way there like the back of our hands and joined the queues of people outside. They were queued all the way around the stadium and back to the Stanley Park car park, all carrying flowers to lay on the pitch.

We just stood in the queue and waited our turn, and when we finally got inside we walked along the front of the main stand and onto the Kop, where we placed our flowers. I sat down on the ground in the spot where the girls used to stand, and looked out on the pitch, at a sea of flowers that reached all the way to the halfway line, and I sobbed. I'd never seen anything like it. A Salvation Army man came over and asked if we were a bereaved family, and then told us the club had set up a place for the families to have tea and coffee, and a private place to sit. He came with us, and showed us to the Players' Lounge, where we found members of the clergy, players and their wives. There I first met Marina Dalglish, wife of the Liverpool manager Kenny, and she sat with us. It was still only four days after the girls had died.

A Catholic priest came to sit with us and I asked him where Sarah and Vicki were. His answer has stayed with me to this day: 'In my Father's house there are many mansions.'

Lovely memories of Yarm school. I'm sitting on the front row, far right, in the cardigan my Aunty Lizzie handknitted for me.

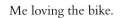

Me loving the bike.

Uncle Tommy looking proud on my wedding day.

They grew up
so fast. In all
photos on this
page: Sarah
(left) and
Vicki (right)

The girls in their
Haberdashers'
uniform. Sarah
(left), Vicki (right)

All of us sitting
together on our
holiday in Spain,
1988.

Vicki (right) looking
tanned after our holiday,
sitting with my brother
David and his then fiancée.

Brave, heroic Liverpool fans carrying my daughter Sarah on a hoarding. Desperately trying to save her life. I can never, ever thank them enough for their efforts.
(Sarah wasn't alone.)

Floral tributes on the pitch at Anfield, 1989.

Vicki (left) and Sarah (right) at home on the school holidays, 1988. Around seven months before the Hillsborough game.

Sarah and Vicki's resting place, April 1989. Fans still leave scarves and notes by their grave, to show their support for our fight for justice.

Mark (left) and Steve (right) were close friends of Sarah's at university and carried her coffin at her funeral.

Me (to the right, in a white hat) standing behind the queen when she visited the Hillsborough memorial at Anfield. I remember how visibly moved she was as she read all the names. Afterwards, she turned to me and said 'They're all so young.'

Screening of Jimmy McGovern's drama documentary *Hillsborough* at the BAFTA Theatre in London, December 1996.

Me and my especially close friend Rachel on the ferry crossing the Mersey to attend the Freedom of the City on the Wirral.

Woman of the Year Award 2016, to recognise the efforts of all the Hillsborough women fighting for justice.

Chrissy (left), Lou (centre) and me (right) being interviewed outside Preston Crown Court in 2019.

From left to right: Deanna, Chrissy, Debbie and me outside the Lowry Court, Salford Quays, 2021. A heartbreaking end to the long road seeking accountability for our loved ones.

My beautiful girls: Sarah
(above) and Vicki (right)

Proud mum.

Much later, I learned it was from John 14:2, a bible verse. He couldn't give me the straight answer I wanted, nobody could. But I felt comforted all the same.

After two hours at Anfield, we decided that, before driving back to London, we would go to the halls of residence and collect Sarah's things. It was one of the hardest things I ever had to do after she passed away. It was still springtime and sunny, and there were daffodils outside her window, in the Carnatic grounds.

When Trevor and I got to D17, Sarah's room, friends had tied a pretty bunch of daffodils with a black lace ribbon around them on her door. The porter, who came up with us, let us in. When he opened that door, I expected to see Sarah standing there, as she always had been when we drove up at weekends to take her to a home game. But not today; she wasn't there. Nor would be ever again. That thought really hit me, and the pain was unbearable.

The porter then let Sarah's friends Linda and Sharla know we were there, and they came along and we sat on Sarah's bed and cried together. I opened Sarah's cupboard in the corner, it was still full of food. So much for her starving away from home – I used to do more shopping for Sarah when she was there than I did for the rest of us! We left the food in a big box on reception, so any of the students who wanted anything could take it, and Sharla and Linda took one of Sarah's mugs each as a memory of their time spent there with her.

There is not a single part of that final trip to Sarah's room at the halls that I don't remember, although trying to explain how I dealt with it is an entirely different matter. The number of people who have said to me, 'I don't know how I would cope if it happened to me. How on earth did you manage?'

The answer is, I don't know. I know that the love of my daughters has helped me. My favourite saying now is, 'I have friends in higher places.'

But I think when most things in life come along, no matter how unimaginably difficult and appalling, you just somehow, some way, have to find your own way of getting from one moment to another.

Funerals have always held an element of fear, doom and gloom for me. I guess that goes back to my granny and grandad's funerals, where as a child I hadn't witnessed any celebration, even though they'd both lived long and happy lives. There was no joy in them, and I wanted to celebrate my girl's lives. I remembered what Sarah had said only two weeks earlier about the music she wanted at her funeral. It would be years before it became the standard thing to have rock music at funerals, but if Sarah wanted it, I was going to make sure she got it. A few days after our visit to the Liverpool cemetery, the minister from our local church came to my house to finalise the arrangements. I told him I wanted 'With or Without You' by U2 played for Sarah, and 'In an Ideal World' by the Christians for Vicki. It took him a moment before he replied.

'Yes, well,' he said, 'I'll have to speak to the church elders about that and decide what is appropriate.'

Appropriate? Given the way the girls had died, and that Sarah had been baptised at the church and my girls had gone to Sunday school there, I was incensed.

'Well,' I said, 'I'm telling you now if you won't do it, I'll go somewhere else – and somewhere else, and somewhere else – until I find a church that will give me the funeral my daughter wanted. So, the choice is yours.'

Later that week, a Church of England vicar from our local church in Hatch End came round on his bike with a message from the Bishop of St Albans to say he would come and officiate at the girls' service if we'd like him too. Trevor and I had never heard of him before, but I imagine the bishop had seen my girls splashed all over the media.

'No thank you,' I told him, 'my daughters go to the Baptist church, but if the bishop would like to come down, he can take part in the service.'

The vicar and Trevor looked at each other open-mouthed. They couldn't believe I'd turned the bishop down, though I did invite him and the vicar to the service. But it was simply that I wanted the girls put to rest in the way they would have wanted to be – and that was more important than who officiated. In the event, the service went ahead in our local church after the minister finally conceded to what I'd asked for, though neither the Church of England vicar nor the bishop chose to attend.

With the post-mortems of all ninety-four supporters who died on the day going on in Sheffield, the coroner's office had to appeal for other pathologists to assist. Trevor was on the phone to the coroner's office several times a day, trying to find out when we could collect the girls and bring them home, while the undertakers were practically screaming for information from them so that they could finalise the funeral arrangements, but nothing was forthcoming. I hated the girls

being up there on their own, in a cold, clinical environment where they knew no one, and I began to go and sit in
their wardrobes where, pulling the sliding doors to, I would
cuddle and smell their clothes. Trevor wouldn't know where
I was at first and later possibly struggled with it, but I had to
do whatever brought me closer to the girls and might help
ease the pain.

Then, six days after the match, on Friday, 21 April, we
finally got the news that we'd been waiting for: the coroner
was releasing the girls' bodies that day. The undertakers
drove to Sheffield to collect them and take them back to the
chapel of rest, where the undertaker's wife dressed them in
their favourite clothes, which I had supplied. I couldn't wait
to welcome the girls home from their terrible ordeal and to
have them back with me, in their own surroundings again.

Typically, funeral directors have to ensure it is appropriate
to bring bodies back to a house, and I think they would
have preferred the girls to stay in the chapel of rest until
their funeral on the following Monday, but I told them
no, all Sarah and Vicki did was go to a football match and
now they had to come home from that match. So, on the
Saturday morning, one week after we had all set out for
that disastrous match, I looked out of the window and saw
two hearses arriving. Although this was one of the saddest
days of my life, I was also excited to have the girls home.

'The girls are back!' I called upstairs to Trevor. 'The girls
have come home!'

I knew immediately by the size of the coffins which one
was Vicki's and which one was Sarah's, as Sarah was several
inches taller than Vicki. I'd got my daughters back and we

asked for them to be taken up to their bedrooms, where their coffins were opened. I then lifted my beautiful daughters up, first Sarah and then Vicki. I hugged them, kissed their gorgeous faces. Then I did their hair and make-up for them, as I knew how they would have liked it. I noticed one of Sarah's hands was black from her knuckles down to the ends of her fingers. Later, when the post-mortem results came in, I asked my GP to explain this to me. He said that this was from where her blood circulation had been cut off for a period of time as she'd desperately tried to hold on to Vicki when she'd fainted during the crush. On the video tape I was to view of the match at the second inquests held in Warrington some twenty-five years later, this was found to have been from 2.45 that afternoon, fifteen minutes before kick-off. It must have been agony for Sarah, battling all that time to keep Vicki from going under in the crowd. I gently tucked Sarah's elegant, blackened hand under the sleeve of her flying jacket. I knew that even if Sarah had a chance of getting out of that crush, she would never have left Vicki to save herself.

I hugged my daughters to me again, then, to make sure they would not be on their own, Trevor and I stayed up all night with them. We sat with one of the girls each, then swapped over every hour or so. The girls were home, if only for a few days, and I felt relieved.

Earlier in the evening, Lara, a close friend of Sarah's from Haberdashers', had come down from St Albans to inquire about the service.

'Will the girls be leaving for the service from the chapel of rest?' she asked.

I said, 'Oh no, they'll be leaving from here. They're upstairs now.'

She was so excited that Sarah was home and asked if she could go up and see her. Lara, like Sarah, had only just turned nineteen, so I said I thought she should go home and have a word with her parents first, and if she still wanted to see Sarah, she should come back with them. This was Lara's first experience of death and I didn't want her to drive back to St Albans that night unaccompanied. Lara went home, and the next morning she was back on the doorstep at 9 a.m. with her father.

Soon after, word got round that the girls were at home and many of their friends and their parents arrived at the house and were going up and down the stairs throughout the day to pay them love and respect. It helped Trevor and me to be occupied: we all reminisced about Sarah and Vicki, and it lifted my soul for a while to hear how much they were both so loved. People were eating food and drinking tea, but I hadn't a clue who was providing it. It was all just happening around me. People stayed until midnight, and during this time one of Sarah's ex-boyfriends came and sat with her, holding her hand. Before he went, he placed a red rose in her hand, along with the cross and rosary someone else had placed there. The next day would be the girls' funeral service in North Harrow.

Chapter 18

It was Monday, 24 April, the morning of the girls' funerals, and I decided to wear an outfit that Sarah had liked when I'd worn it on her nineteenth birthday just two weeks earlier. We'd all gone to Cranks vegetarian restaurant in Covent Garden and then to see Willy Russell's *Blood Brothers* musical. I also remembered the conversation we'd had when she'd talked about her own death, and she said she didn't want any black, and no tears. It was a navy jacket with a thin purple stripe through it, and a long skirt. I knew instinctively that Sarah would have wanted me to wear it.

When Chris and Jeff arrived that morning, Chris gave me this strange look. I was puzzled and asked her, 'Do I look all right?'

'Yes,' she replied. 'But look at your feet.'

When I looked down, I realised I had odd shoes on, both black, but different styles. It was still such a huge effort to get showered and dressed that I hadn't noticed, and neither had Trevor. But it showed my state of mind, and I really didn't know how I was going to get through the service.

The cortège set out from the house, Sarah's hearse and then Vicki's, as it was the protocol for the elder sibling to lead. I wondered what all these police cars and motorbikes were doing alongside us but realised, with all the local and media interest, the police felt it necessary to give us an escort, and outriders would stop at every traffic light to hold back the traffic so we could pass through. It was surreal, like the whole place had come to a standstill. The cortège drove past our old house in Pinner, where we had arranged to pause for a moment because we'd been so happy there. It wasn't the most direct route, but it was almost a journey of the girls' life, and full of happy memories. We paused again at Longfield school, where the girls had gone before Haberdashers'. And I thought of Mr Brignall, the head teacher, and of Vicki doing such a warm and funny impression of him taking assembly while rattling the loose change in his pocket.

As we went down into North Harrow all the roads were closed, and the traffic had been halted for us until we arrived at the Baptist church, where there was a crowd of people standing outside. We were expecting a good number of people to turn up, and once we got inside the little church was packed, including some fifty students who'd come down on a coach from Liverpool University that morning. There were so many people, they had to stand in the side rooms where they held things like the Sunday School meetings, while other people had to stand outside the church by the entrance. I knew the girls were popular, and this was a wonderful testament to them. As the coffins were carried in, U2's 'With or Without You' played out into the church, followed by the Christians 'In an Ideal World'. I looked at the coffins placed side by side in the church – my girls were still together, even now – and as I listened to their music playing, all of their fun and laughter came back to me. How I missed that. But I didn't cry. I was in too much pain, and Sarah had requested no tears.

As we walked out of the church, first Sarah's coffin and then Vicki's coffin, then Trevor and me, the girls were carried out to the Liverpool anthem 'You'll Never Walk Alone'.

Everyone was invited back to the wake at the house afterwards. We had no idea how many people to expect, but the house and gardens were overflowing with the girls' friends and everyone else. People filled every room and even stood on the stairs chatting, everyone remembering the girls.

It actually was a fitting celebration of the girls' lives. It was at the wake I met two close friends of Sarah's from uni: eighteen-year-old Steve, who had come down on the coach for the funeral, and nineteen-year-old Mark. In the six short months Sarah had been at uni she had spoken so frequently about Steve and Mark that I felt I already knew them, and when I met them for the first time at the wake, I threw my arms around them.

'People were thrown together in these most difficult of circumstances,' as Steve said later, 'and we were all talking about the girls and getting to know each other.'

I knew that if Sarah could choose, she wouldn't want the funeral directors carrying her coffin at the burial in Liverpool the following day, so I asked Steve and Mark if they would do it. Given that they were just two young men at the time, I now realise how unfair it was of me to have put them on the spot like that. But I was so grateful they agreed to do it.

Trevor and I didn't want strangers carrying Vicki's coffin either, but Trevor didn't feel it was right to carry one of his daughters' coffins and not the other, which I understood. So, it was arranged for Vicki's uncle – my brother David – to carry her, along with her uncle Barry, and I felt she would have been ok with that.

At the wake, two other close friends of Sarah from uni – Sharla and Rebecca – came over and asked me if they could see Sarah's room. I took them upstairs and we sat on Sarah's bed. I hadn't touched the girls' rooms, I just couldn't face it. Everything was exactly as they'd left it. Even the sheets hadn't been washed, so I could still smell Sarah on them.

I told the girls that Sarah had been home for a few days before the funeral. 'Home?' one of them asked. 'You mean after the post-mortems?' 'Yes,' I said. They were very upset and asked, 'But why didn't you let us know? We would have loved to have seen Sarah.'

The three of them had been expecting to go out on the Sunday night when Sarah got back to Liverpool after the semi-final. At the time I wasn't able to think about it or anything else outside of the girls, but now I recognise how important seeing a deceased loved one can be to help people come to terms with a sudden death.

Sharla and Rebecca wanted to know what clothes Sarah would be buried in and I said I had dressed her in her gorgeous leather flying jacket, which we had bought her for Christmas. They were so pleased as they knew how much she loved it. I learned so much about grief from this conversation, and how important it would have been for them to see Sarah and say goodbye properly.

After the wake, Graham, a friend of Trevor's from work, offered to come down to London on the train and drive us and my brothers back to his home in St Helens, near Liverpool. It was an extraordinary act of kindness. When we arrived, his wife Barbara had prepared dinner for us and arranged overnight accommodation for us at their home and at their next-door neighbours', Norma and Mike, who kindly provided accommodation for several members of Trevor's close family too.

The following day, Tuesday, 25 April, the girls were to be buried. The funeral directors had arranged for the cortège to stop off at a little Methodist church in the iconic Penny Lane of the Beatles song, where the minister had arranged a short service. The girls thought the Beatles and Liverpool culture was great and would have loved this idea. The minister gave a blessing and said some lovely words about the girls, then we set off again with a full police escort along roads which had been closed off to traffic, and all the traffic lights were set to red.

We didn't know anyone in Liverpool, and I didn't expect there to be many people at the burial, apart from close friends and family. But as we approached, crowds of people had turned out to line the streets of Allerton and bowed their heads as a mark of respect as we passed through on the way to the cemetery. It was surreal: I couldn't take my eyes off the hearses in front. Each had a wreath with my daughters' names written in flowers.

'Who are these people?' I asked Trevor, but he had no more idea than me. Later, we were told people had come from all over the city, as well as Liverpool fans who had read about us burying our girls today and had come out to support us. Quite a few people who had attended the service the day before in London also came up to the burial. We were surprised and so deeply touched by the wonderful outpouring of love for our girls, and the tremendous support people gave us. We really were not walking alone.

As the cortège went up the driveway to Allerton Cemetery, there was a mix of mourners dressed in sombre black and people in LFC football shirts and scarves, and hundreds more people lined the way and stood by the open graveside. Kenny Dalglish's wife Marina was there, alongside Liverpool striker and local boy John Aldridge, and Dorothy Gavin, the Mayor of Liverpool in the full chains of office and regalia. Trevor had made a deal with the media that while they could film and record the funeral service in London, there were to be no cameras at the cemetery and the burial was private.

'It felt like the eyes of the world were on us,' Steve remarked. 'We were pallbearing in front of all of this, and I had never done it before. But because of the tightly packed crowd around the graveside there was a very narrow walkway to the grave, and the whole time I was worried about slipping and dropping the coffin into that chasm in the ground.'

With hindsight I can see it was a big responsibility for a couple of young men as Steve and Mark were, but they did Sarah proud that day. I later learned that Steve had had to borrow black clothes from his fellow students for the task. At the graveside before the burial, Trevor thanked everyone for coming, and surprisingly, the crowd burst into applause.

Marina Dalglish and John Aldridge stood side by side with me and Trevor as Sarah and Vicki were lowered into the ground. I don't know how I stood there and watched that, but I think I was just totally numb by then. Suddenly it got all too much for John, who picked me up and squeezed me so tightly, I could hardly breathe. John was sobbing and declaring football was never worth this. He is a local boy who, like my girls, had been a supporter of the club since childhood. I stressed to him that neither Sarah nor Vicki would want him to give up football, I was certain of that, and told John if they knew that it would make them very sad. I still count John and his beautiful wife Joan as very good friends. He was so badly affected by Hillsborough and, although it must have been very difficult for him, he attended the funerals of many of the victims.

After the burial, we'd arranged for a small reception to be held at Barbara and Graham's. They were both from Liverpool and this was the first time I had ever experienced Scouse hospitality. We had told them to expect at most twenty-five people, but several more turned up. Many of these were Sarah and Vicki's friends who'd been at the service in London the day before and had come up for the burial. Faced with more people than anticipated, Barbara and Graham simply opened up their home to whoever called and, with help from their neighbours Norma and Mike, put on a spread of hot food and drink. Neither couple would take anything for it, and I could see why Sarah wanted to stay on here when she finished her degree.

Along with the fans, these were the same warm, kind and friendly Liverpudlians who were being given a bad name in the press. It just didn't make sense. The *Sun* article 'The Truth' had only a few days earlier been splashed across the front page, which at the time had the biggest circulation in the country. In Liverpool it was boycotted in newsagents and shops across the city and, on occasions, burnt in the streets. The scurrilous lies and smears it perpetuated caused so much hurt to the families and the fans, as well as wreaking damage on the reputation of the city, mud that still sticks to this day. The *Sun* is still, rightly, boycotted in Liverpool and many other places worldwide.

Chapter 19

On 29 April a service was arranged at the Anglican Cathedral in Liverpool for the families of those who had died at Hillsborough. We hadn't been in touch with any of the other families, because we lived in London and they were from various other parts of the country, not just Liverpool.

Some three thousand people were in attendance, including the Liverpool team, the prime minister, Margaret Thatcher, and various other politicians, and the Duke and Duchess of Kent representing the royal family. When I walked into the cathedral with Trevor, the choir were singing and the whole experience nearly blew me away.

David Sheppard, the Anglican Bishop of Liverpool, was airlifted in from a Scottish Isle by an RAF helicopter to attend, and the Catholic Archbishop of Liverpool, Derek Worlock, took the service. Several of the Liverpool team took part in the proceedings, including goalie Bruce Grobbelaar, who had witnessed the crush behind him and helped to get the game stopped. He gave the first reading, and Ronnie Whelan and Steve Nicol carried the communion bread and wine. I have never been one to shed tears, but it was a most moving service and I cried throughout. I remember the choir sang Andrew Lloyd Webber's requiem 'Pie Jesu' as the Book of Remembrance was brought out. It was so beautiful and even now, when I recall it, it moves me to tears.

After the service, four members of each family were invited to go down into the crypt to meet all the dignitaries and important parliamentarians of the time. Trevor, Trevor's mum, my brother David and I went to meet them. Tea and alcohol were served, should you want it, and Margaret Thatcher was doing the rounds. It had just been announced that there would be an inquiry into Hillsborough starting in May, led by Lord Justice Taylor. Of course, Trevor and I welcomed this, but with the *Sun* newspaper having falsely blamed the fans in such a vile and disgusting way, we naturally had our concerns about it. We were aware of the sway that the newspaper had on public opinion and were conscious that we didn't want this to affect the inquiry and its outcomes. So, when the prime minister came over to us, I asked, 'Mrs Thatcher, can you please ensure that the Taylor Inquiry won't be a whitewash?'

She didn't speak for a moment or two but stood looking me up and down. As she did so, I noticed her thick make-up – foundation – that made her resemble a Madame Tussauds waxwork. It looked bizarre and I found this deeply unsettling rather than comforting. She was a good few inches taller than me, and leaning forward to look me in the eye, she put her arm on my shoulder and said in a monotone voice, 'My dear, a mother's place is in the kitchen filling the fridge with food for Christmas.'

I looked at her in shock; I couldn't find the words to reply. Dennis was standing behind her like a nodding dog with his gin and tonic in hand, as if she was saying something wonderful. Then, before I could formulate a response to what she'd said, she moved on to talk to another family.

Here she was, a woman in the top job in the country, telling me a woman's place is in the kitchen? And filling the fridge with food for Christmas? Not only was it April, so Christmas was months away, but when your first Christmas without your children was going to be yet another nightmare, and then to be told it's 'a mother's place' when I had lost my daughters and was no longer a mum? It was breathtakingly insensitive.

I looked at Trevor and the others to try and ascertain if I'd heard her correctly. They looked as confused as I did. While we were still reeling from the prime minister's comments, Neil Kinnock, the leader of the opposition, came over. My shock was now transforming into determination and I said to him, 'Hello, Mr Kinnock, we've just met the prime minister and when I asked her to ensure that the Taylor Inquiry would not be a whitewash, can you explain to us what she meant by this?' And I quoted her words verbatim to him.

He looked as confused as we had, and replied, 'Oh, the woman's head is filled with wires! As leader of the opposition, I have to have important meetings with her about security and other things. If I disagree with her at a meeting, at first she comes over all the pussy,' and he put on this sexy, kittenish look, 'and when that doesn't work, she turns nasty.'

I don't know what those two were on that day, but only two weeks earlier we'd been leading our ordinary lives and had gone to a cup semi-final and lost both our daughters, our only children. We were in the midst of the worst grief imaginable and had just been to a memorial service for our girls and all the victims, and instead of support we had our prime minister talking like that to me, and the leader of the opposition making inappropriate faces. As we left the cathedral that day, all I could think was, *We really have gone down the rabbit hole now. We are with Alice in Wonderland at the Mad Hatter's tea party.*

In the weeks after the funeral, Trevor and I went back to Haberdashers' to discuss a special service for Vicki and Sarah the school was going to hold in the autumn, and to collect Vicki's things from her locker. It was there I met Mrs Wood again, the geography teacher. I told her that what she'd said to Vicki at the A-level evening had brought joy to Vicki's life.

She replied, 'I wasn't just saying that to get Vicki to take A-level geography. She really was brilliant at it, and the person I was talking about did go on to Cambridge, which Vicki would've been able to.'

I was so grateful that Vicki got to know that. And I think even though Trevor and I would play down Sarah's results because Vicki never felt good enough, her big sister knew differently. Sarah tried to tell me how good Vicki was at maths, and said she was in the wrong set and for that reason she didn't get to do GCSE maths a year earlier, as she had done. But Vicki had seemed happy in that set, so I didn't ask to get her moved. However, in a maths test of all pupils in her year to see how far ahead the top group were, Vicki came out with 98 – which was phenomenal, and the top score across all of the sets.

Vicki was always much better than she thought she was, and in some ways Trevor and I possibly bought into the comparison she'd made between herself and Sarah.

When the replay of the semi-final against Nottingham Forest took place three weeks later on 7 May at Old Trafford, I was so pleased that John Aldridge decided to play. He scored two of the Liverpool goals, and Liverpool went on to beat Nottingham Forest 3-2, though Trevor and I could not bear to watch the game and instead went for a walk in the woods near where we lived.

The Football Association then issued four free tickets to the FA Cup Final to each bereaved family, so Trevor and I went. We wanted to go on behalf of the girls, who would have been there, and we took my brother and another of Sarah's friends from uni, Sean Richardson. There was a one-minute silence for the victims of the disaster. I knew that perimeter fencing, where it existed, had been taken down in some grounds around the country, but not all clubs did this immediately or indeed had fencing. But I was in such a dazed state at the cup final, I'm not sure I even noticed at Wembley. I was, however, vaguely aware of other people around me who were looking pretty much in the same state. We had not yet set up the family support group and I did not realise that these were the families of the other Hillsborough victims, and we'd all been seated in one area of the ground.

The cup final was a local derby between Liverpool and Everton, who we beat 3-2 with John Aldridge scoring the first goal, and Rushy (Ian Rush) the other two. As the ball hit the back of the net each time, I thought of Vicki bolting upstairs afterwards, throwing her typewriter on the bed and bashing out that match report. That would have been her last match report ever, as she was about to start at the boutique the following season. But what a report it would have been, what a high to finish on, and the girls would've loved to have seen Ronnie Whelan lifting the cup! Some supporters believed that Liverpool should have been allowed to keep the FA Cup permanently as a tribute to all those who lost their lives or were injured at Hillsborough. But this was never going to happen at the time, while the British public were being led to believe that drunken, loutish supporters were to blame for the disaster. With the reputation all football fans had at the time, the Liverpool fans were perhaps an easy target. But as the lies surrounding the events of Hillsborough grew and were perpetuated in the media, it seemed that only those from Liverpool understood the truth of the matter.

It was some time after the FA Cup final that Trevor and I went on one of our regular trips to Allerton Cemetery to visit Sarah and Vicki's grave. As we were driving along the path towards the grave, we saw a woman standing there, looking at the girls' numerous flowers and wreaths. She was turning to walk away, but the car's central locking system started switching on and off, making a loud noise. She turned, and when she saw us coming, she stopped. We got out of the car, and she asked us who we were. There was no headstone at the grave, but LFC had sent each of the victims' families a football made from flowers, and we had two, one for each of our daughters. She recognised them, because she had been sent one too.

She told us her name was Doreen Jones and that she had lost her beloved son Richard, or Rick as they called him, along with his lovely girlfriend Tracey Cox. Both were in their early twenties and had science degrees from Sheffield University. Doreen came across as a very dignified lady, but I could see the pain she was in – I could see it on her face. Her son was buried just six graves along from our daughters. We talked about what had been said in the *Sun*, and the scurrilous lies that had blackened the names of our children, the other victims who died or were injured that day and the Liverpool fans. Her daughter, Stephanie Jones, had also been at the match, but her version of events, much like ours, did not tally with the police or the press. Trevor said he felt that, given the way things were going, the victims' families were going to get 'shafted'. Doreen looked at us and said, 'You should come and speak to my husband.'

She invited us back to her house near the cemetery and made us a cup of tea, then rang her husband, Les, and put him on the phone to Trevor. After that call, we were all in agreement that we weren't going to get at the truth if we didn't do something.

Unbeknown to us, Billy Pemberton, the father of twenty-three-year-old William Pemberton who had lost his life at Hillsborough, was talking to social services to try to set up a support group for families, to provide a space where they would find emotional support. Trevor and Les wanted something more than tea and sympathy; they realised we had a massive fight on our hands if we were ever to get truth and justice for those who'd died.

Billy had got all the families' addresses from social services, and in July an initial meeting was set up by social services at the Sangster Centre in Stanley Park, Liverpool, to decide the way forward. When we arrived, there were already a lot of people there, and it was agreed that we would combine the two goals: to form a family group to support each other, and to campaign for justice. Because Trevor was a managing director with a lot of experience of chairing meetings, he was voted chair of what became known as the Hillsborough Family Support Group (HFSG).

It was a long way for us to come up to the meetings, but we were coming up to visit the girls' grave every week anyway, and sometimes twice a week in the early days.

LFC worked closely with the HFSG, which represented the majority of the families, and they still do. It must have been difficult for them to satisfy all the different families' needs, as each family's needs would be individual to them, but I guess they tried to do their best.

From the outset, the HFSG wasn't all plain sailing. How could it be with so many families all bereaved and in shock, and with different ideas on how best to approach our need for truth and justice for our loved ones? Though truth and justice we could all agree on, after a while a small number of families left because they thought that Trevor was handling HFSG affairs too much like a business. He wanted an approach where we did not play into the press's hands by fitting the stereotype they and the police had created and smeared the Liverpool fans with; the focus was on making it a campaigning group. Others wanted a tougher approach, and they went on to continue the fight for justice outside of the group. When confronted about it in a meeting, Trevor was firmly of the opinion that the HFSG should take the dignified route.

'That's how we're going to beat this lot.'

I understood Trevor's reasoning and I agreed with that approach, and that dignity is still recognised today. However, we needed to be tough and to fight in a dignified way. It has taken over thirty years to get to where we are, and no one should have to fight this long for truth and some semblance of justice. No one. And the same goes for accountability, as without accountability there can be no justice. If those in authority are not accountable for their actions, it places every citizen in this country in danger.

Chapter 20

After five weeks, Trevor was keen to get back to his old work routine, living in Dudley during the week. But I knew I was incapable of living in the house on my own all week with Trevor away. It was just too much, too soon. I pleaded with him to work from home. After all, he was only an hour and a half's drive up the motorway. Even if he reduced it to a couple of nights away a week, it would have helped me to cope. But Trevor would never agree to that. He needed to go, but I needed him to be home more often now.

We'd reached an impasse. The compromise was that my brother David and his girlfriend Dolores would move in with me, so I wouldn't be on my own. They arrived the night before Trevor went back to work. They were quite happy to do this, as they'd been renting a single room in a friend's house. Dolores got home from work by five and my brother, a milkman at that time, was always home in the afternoons when I got back from work.

After Trevor went, I began sleeping in the girls' beds at night, so I could smell them on their still unwashed sheets, and I continued to do so for many weeks. In the mornings, David never knew which bed he'd find me in. I'd decided I wasn't going to take those sheets off their beds and wash them ever again. It was many weeks before I finally gave in.

Sarah's clothes were in a big, fitted wardrobe, and some-times I would sit on the floor and smell the clothes hanging down. Vicki's wardrobe was smaller, but I still liked to get in there and have a good smell and hug the clothes. It was the closest I could get to giving them a hug. It might seem strange behaviour, but it gave me comfort and a closeness to them.

Three months after the disaster, on 1 August 1989, Lord Justice Taylor's interim report* came out, setting out his find-ings from the inquiry into Hillsborough. This blamed South Yorkshire Police (SYP) for the disaster and not the fans. Both Trevor and I had attended the inquiry, as Trevor was asked to give evidence of our experiences on the day. One of the things Taylor was highly critical of was the police failure to close the tunnel when pens 3 and 4 were full by 2.50 p.m.; that access should have been closed off whether gate C was to be opened or not. He went on to say it should have been clear in the control room, where there was a view of the pens and of the crowd at the turnstiles, that the tunnel had to be closed:

> If orders had been given to that effect when gate C was opened, the fans could have been directed to the empty areas of the wings and this disaster could still have been avoided. Failure to give that order was a blunder of the first magnitude.[†]

---

* Taylor's final report was published in January 1990. 'Lord Taylor's final report on the Hillsborough stadium disaster', Her Majesty's Stationery Office, January 1990.

† Taylor (1990), p. 40.

Taylor also criticised senior commanding officers as being 'defensive and evasive witnesses' who refused to accept any responsibility for their mistakes:

It is a matter of regret that at the hearing, and in their submissions, the South Yorkshire Police were not prepared to concede they were in any respect at fault in what occurred . . . the police case was to blame the fans for being late and drunk . . .

. . . Such an unrealistic approach gives cause for anxiety as to whether lessons have been learnt. It would have been more seemly and encouraging for the future if responsibility had been faced.*

The inquiry also found there was 'no provision' for controlling and filtering the entry of supporters into the small and 'awkward' turnstile area. The Chief Constable of SYP, Peter Wright, CBE, said he fully accepted the findings of the report, and despite me and Trevor and many other families having feared the worst with the Taylor Inquiry, it made us feel that the authorities were dealing with the disaster appropriately. We felt optimistic that justice would prevail and looked forward to the next stage when the Crown Prosecution Service would begin prosecutions against the police and others responsible for us losing our loved ones.

With the new season starting soon after this, Trevor and I began going to the matches again. As chair of the HFSG,

---

* Taylor (1989), p. 50.

Trevor held regular meetings with Peter Robinson, the Chief Executive of LFC, after the games, and I started to wait for him in the director's bar.

By now Trevor was fully back to work, and he was going back up to his flat in Dudley every Sunday night, or sometimes straight after Sunday lunch, as he tried to carry on as before. He thought we could have the same lifestyle as when the girls were alive, and for him it was the same lifestyle that he'd had up there for the last four years. Had he worked in London, and been home in the evenings, it would have been a different matter. This would have meant we both had more time to help each other cope with our inconceivable loss.

The college where I worked had been very understanding. When I'd contacted the head, she told me to stay off for as long as I needed, and not to worry about a sick note. They kept me on full pay throughout. The education department at the London Borough of Harrow weren't putting pressure on me to return, and I knew that I really wasn't ready to go back – and yet I went back to work after six weeks, because it seemed to be what Trevor expected of me. I did my best, and I only managed it because the college made it so easy for me.

The problem with going back to work was that it involved a relatively short drive, and I struggled driving an empty car now, without the girls. I used to drive them everywhere in my car, and hated being in there without them. Trevor used to say to me, 'Make them catch the bus like other kids, instead of mollycoddling them!' I admit I was like their private taxi service – but I enjoyed that, and the chats we'd have in the car and the music we'd listen to on the radio.

I know it might sound ridiculous but, now they'd gone, I couldn't face getting into the car. There were so many memories there for me. This was until one day when Trevor said to me in no uncertain terms, 'When you go back to work, you will need to be able to drive your car. I'll come to the college with you, and you can drive.'

So I did, even though I was crying. When we arrived at my department, two of the teachers I usually worked with were there. They looked oddly at me, then one of them said, 'Jenni, are you sure you are ready to come back? You don't have to – the head understands.'

Trevor didn't say anything. But I knew how he felt. The school suggested it would be easier for me to do a gradu-ated return, depending on how I felt on a day-by-day basis.

'If you turn up at nine o'clock in the morning and you want to go home at quarter past nine or ten o'clock, just say to us, "I can't do this today."'

So I started to work for an hour or two a day, and then go home. In time I managed to increase how long I was able to stay. Sarah had a collection of badges with sayings on them. One was huge with 'Leave me alone, I'm having a crisis' written on it. I'd wear that to work if I needed them to know, and the college had a large walk-in storage cupboard in the classroom where I worked. It was huge, almost like another room, used for storing books and stationery. If everything was getting too much for me, I could use that for privacy at any time. I would sit in there for as long as it took to feel better.

Finally, I began taking an interest in what I looked like again: my clothes, hair and make-up became the armour I put on to get out there and face the world again. It was my protection as I tried to get on with things, which is what I knew the girls would want me to do. Putting on my armour always took a long time, which I had to factor into my morning routine, but it had to be done as I was going out there and representing the girls. I still wear my armour today.

When I was more comfortable driving again, sometimes I'd find myself sitting at a traffic light and another car would pull up alongside with a family in it, or I'd pass a mother driving her kids to school the way I used to, and I would feel really envious. It was because Sarah and Vicki were not there, and I couldn't get used to that world. I wanted my normality back. The new world I was living in was just too hard.

One of the most difficult times for me was the late afternoon, from 4 p.m. to 6 p.m.: coming-home-from-school time. That was when I was at my most restless. I used to ask my brother David to go down to the bus stop every afternoon – because although I took Vicki to school each morning, she would come back on the Haberdasher's coach, which got into Hatch End at four-thirty each afternoon. I would say to David, 'Would you just go down to the bus stop and make sure Vicki doesn't get off the coach?'

At first, he used to say, 'OK then,' and off he'd go and stay out for the appropriate length of time, which must have been horrendously stressful for him. This went on for weeks and weeks, and he would come back and assure me, 'No, she didn't get off.' Then one day, before he went, he said to me, 'You do know she *isn't* going to get off the coach, don't you?' I nodded, but I still sent him out – just in case.

Years later when we spoke about it, he said, 'Don't you think if I, as a thirty-something bloke at the time, had been hanging round a bus stop watching all those girls getting off the school coach every day, that their parents might have had something to say? Or the school? Or even the police?'

I had never even thought about that. All that was in my head was that somebody had to be there to meet Vicki off the school coach. Long after that, whenever I saw a Hearn's coach with all the girls in their Haberdashers' uniforms on board, my heart would turn over, and that same pain would hit me again. With hindsight, I realise I was being completely irrational in those early days, just trying to survive. My friends accepted it. The only person who didn't was my husband. He wanted me to be the same Jenni without the girls as I had been with them. But sadly, he wanted the impossible.

When he came home, I don't think Trevor liked David and Dolores being there. When he came back Friday nights, it was to a sparkling clean home, a fridge full of food and all his shirts washed and ironed, ready to take back on a Sunday evening, just as it had always been – though none of this was down to me now, but to Dolores and David. Dolores used to iron all Trevor's shirts and my brother would go shopping. 'What do you want today?' he'd ask, and I'd say, 'Oh, look in the cupboard and see if there's anything we need.' I had been house-proud before the tragedy, but now I'd lost all interest in the home. Dolores, however, loved playing house, so the place was spotless.

And there was Trevor coming home at the weekend and complaining about them being there.

I reminded him, 'I wouldn't survive without them, and you would be coming back to a very different home.'

They were my safety net and we were very fortunate to have them, but when Trevor came home at weekends, he wanted to have me and the house all to himself. But you can't always have everything you want, and I think the tension began building between us at this point.

I didn't know if I would survive the loss of my daughters, and I didn't know if I even wanted to. I had known loss before because I had lost both my grandparents early on, who were the closest thing I had to parents, but this was something completely different and the pain was unbelievable. However, I hated people offering me platitudes like, 'They are two little angels in heaven now,' even though they were only trying to help. At the Sunday school at the Wesleyan chapel I attended as a child in Yarm, they'd say, 'Bad things don't happen to good people.' At a young age I was taken in by this, but now, over thirty years later, I realised bad things did happen, no matter what kind of people you were.

Feeling disillusioned with my Christian faith, in the first few months after Hillsborough I researched every religion I could think of, as this heaven-and-hell scenario and the girls floating up on a cloud wasn't good enough. I thought they would be bored stiff up there, and it didn't reassure me in any way.

I started to go to Hatch End library and get books out on other religions to see what I could glean from them. We had Hindu neighbours, Jewish families and Muslims too. Whenever anyone came to the house to offer their condolences and Trevor went out to the kitchen to make them tea, I would straight away quiz them about their beliefs: 'Where do you think Sarah and Vicki are now? What do you think they are doing?'

I might have alarmed one or two of them or made them feel uncomfortable, but I didn't notice. One day Trevor took me aside and said, 'You know, you're going to have to stop doing this, Jenni.'

And I thought, *Yes, I probably am.* But by that point I'd discovered elements of spiritualism, Buddhism and Hinduism that I particularly liked: reincarnation and souls recognising each other from past lives. I do think that animals have souls, which the Christian religion doesn't. Sarah had become a vegetarian in her teens, and we would talk about animals being sentient beings and how they could feel pain and love, and become depressed, and yes, I could see that.

One day my brother, who knew I was interested in aspects of spiritualism, came home and said he'd found a little spiritualist church in Harrow. So the following week, David, Dolores and I snuck in at the back during a spiritualist service, as if we were doing something wrong – like going devil-worshipping or something! But it turned out to be the most beautiful service, and the message I got was that while we are all grieving, the spiritual family of those who have died are welcoming them home. It wasn't about if the girls were good, they would get to see their family again, and if they were bad, they would burn in hell. I had learned as a child that religion can be terrifying, and later that for some it can be a source of solace, but any element or branch of philosophy, culture or religion that gave me comfort regarding my girls whereabouts at the time, I'd hang on to it for as long as necessary. But soon I would find other methods to help me to cope.

Something that reinforced my belief in spirits happened months later. Steve was staying with us and, after a meal at the local pub, we were back at the house and he suggested playing a game of Trivial Pursuit.

I still had the original game that Sarah, Vicki, Trevor and I would play as a family. We used to play it a lot and we loved it. So Steve sat on the floor on one side of the board and I sat on the other, and I set it all up. We were about to start playing, when Steve suddenly went into a coughing and sneezing fit, this went on for ages. When he managed to stop for a moment, he asked, 'What perfume have you just put on?'

I said, 'Steve, I have never been out of the room – when have I been spraying perfume on myself? I have been setting up the game. I can't smell anything.'

But he was all red in the face and choking at this point. When he stopped choking and the fit went, it was my turn. I was suddenly covered in perfume, and I started coughing and sneezing. After a short while, the smell disappeared, and I said, 'I can't smell it now.'

Steve replied, 'Yes, it's gone.'

The air had cleared, but I realised what the smell was and I went up to Sarah's bedroom, which was still exactly as she'd left it, and took the bottle of perfume she'd got from the Body Shop back downstairs with me. I didn't say anything to Steve, but sprayed it on his arm and asked if that was what he could smell. He said, 'That's it! How did you know?'

'Because it's Sarah's White Musk perfume,' I replied.

The colour drained from his face. Steve was a scientist, but there was no rational explanation to what was happening. Without playing a single round, we packed the Trivial Pursuit game away, and the trail of White Musk disappeared.

I thought, *Sarah, you may not be playing Trivial Pursuit with us, but you are definitely playing games.*

Chapter 21

I have been very fortunate with the people whose paths have crossed with mine after the disaster, and this is thanks to my daughters. Since Hillsborough I don't think there was anyone in Liverpool that was not affected in some way, either by friend or family losing their life in the tragedy, or a colleague or friend of a friend. You talk about Hillsborough and everyone remembers where they were when it happened, everyone has a story. It is part of Liverpool history now, part of the structure of Liverpool life. And for Sarah's friends at Liverpool uni, they were at the heart of it too.

After the girls' funerals, people had expected me to just get back to normal and get on with my life. If only it could have been that easy. The loneliness and the loss only really start to kick in at this point, while the reality and pain gets worse after the funeral. But one of the saving graces for me was to keep in touch with Mark, Steve, Sharla and the others. In those few weeks after the funeral, when Trevor and I visited the girls' graves, we always tried to call in on Sarah's friends in the halls of residence and invite them out to eat before we drove back to London. Mark and Steve were so full of life and laughter, which was missing in our lives since the girls had gone, and Sharla particularly needed to talk about Sarah as much as I needed to listen. We were all bereaved.

Sharla and I would spend a lot of time talking about Sarah – we needed that as we tried to get through. On occasion I would stay at Sharla's house, and we'd lie on her huge bed in the dark and talk all night about Sarah. I heard stories about Mark and Steve being dressed as skeletons all in black, and Sarah and the girls painted all over in green, dressed as tree witches. I knew from our phone calls that Sarah was fond of Mark, who had later emerged from her room with green face paint all over him! Like a kid with chocolate round its mouth who had been caught eating what he shouldn't! I wasn't surprised and it made me smile. I also learned from her friends that she continued to battle against social injustice and challenged sexism, racism and disablism whenever she saw it. That made me proud.

As well as her own friends, Vicki was missed by Sarah's friends too. I knew she was a great mimic and Mark told me stories of how she very quickly mastered his Nottingham accent, having them all in stitches. Mark was impressed by her skills, as unlike a Manchester or Yorkshire accent, few people were able to accomplish a Nottingham accent as Vicki had done. I was glad she had made them laugh too, just as she had me and Sarah crease up at home. I think she would have made a great mimic. I'm told that is why she was so good at languages, because she had a good ear.

Trevor and I invited all of Sarah's friends to stay at our home in London once the academic year ended, which the boys chose to do – coming down at weekends on a regular basis. Because it was a hot summer, Trevor would do a barbecue for us all on the patio.

'I've got so many memories of us there,' Steve recalled. He would occasionally come down for a couple of days midweek too.

It was a relief to have the boys around, and a relief for David and Delores to have someone else there too. They had the ability to lift my spirits, albeit only for a short while. Whenever Steve visited, music and laughter arrived too, and he would do Tommy Cooper impressions, make jokes and keep fit by hanging by his arms from the garage rafters and lifting me up to do the same – though, being so small, I would get stuck and we would end up laughing until Steve helped me down! Steve had no inhibitions, and he made me realise, even in the midst of this awful adversity, it was OK to feel whatever I was feeling: to laugh or to cry. And that I didn't need to follow any conventional behaviour. I could do whatever kept my head above water and kept me going. As Mark said, 'We didn't really know what else to do [to help Jenni] apart from try to have a laugh and have fun. We weren't going to sit down and have some big conversation about it, we didn't have the life experience to do that. All we knew was to try to live in the moment.'

And that suited me too. If somebody had asked me, 'What shall we do this evening?' I couldn't think that far ahead. All I knew was, 'I'm here now, but I don't know how or where I'm going to be in five minutes' time.'

So living – or existing – in the moment was my survival technique, and I guess it helped the boys too, who were also bereaved. Later in the summer, Steve went off to work for Camp America for the rest of the holidays and Mark, who

was working in London, continued to visit us on the occa-
sional weekend.

In June 1989, Trevor and I attended the mini-inquests on
our daughters, held at a medico-legal centre in Sheffield.
Evidence was given by the pathologists who performed
the post-mortems, confirming the time and cause of death,
and families were given the opportunity to meet whichever
pathologist performed your loved one's post-mortem. This
meant two pathologists in Sarah and Vicki's cases, as they'd
had different ones. The mini-inquests were formal and
matter-of-fact; you were given a time to attend and it was
all concluded in an hour or so in our case. If other families
were there, I don't remember seeing them.

Not long after we'd arrived I saw Graham McCombie,
our designated family liaison officer from West Midlands
Police. He was a lovely man and visited us regularly after
the girls' passed. I'd told him about Willy Russell's musical,
Blood Brothers, which was on in the West End, which we'd
attended as family five days before the disaster and really
loved. Graham then went to see it and told us he really
enjoyed it, and saw it again numerous times. We'd seen
plenty of Graham, and he would often call in when he
was passing and bring flowers, and have tea and cake with
David, Dolores and me. Graham also gave me a bleeper to
ring him on day or night if I needed help, but here he was
now in the court lobby, unable to look me in the eye. He
seemed distant and uncomfortable when he spoke to me. I
couldn't understand it, though I would later on, when the
main inquest started.

I was shocked when on 30 August, a few short weeks after the mini-inquests were adjourned, I heard on the ITV news that the Crown Prosecution Service (CPS) had announced they'd found 'insufficient evidence' to justify bringing criminal proceedings against anybody from any organisation for any offence arising out of the deaths. I'd felt quietly confident after Lord Justice Taylor's findings earlier in the month that the police at the very least would be prosecuted. But every part of me ached when I heard this. I could not believe it. Despite all the damning findings of the Taylor Inquiry, which the Chief Constable Peter Wright had fully accepted, and with what we'd seen ourselves that day, how could that possibly be right? We'd been lulled into a false sense of security after Taylor, while the CPS decision not to hold anyone to account for the ninety-five deaths nearly tipped me over the edge. Though I realised then this was only the start of the fight.

After that, things moved fast. As chair of HFSG, Trevor was on the TV news more and more, and we were in Liverpool every weekend. At noon every Sunday we'd go to Allerton Cemetery, and then onto the HFSG meetings. Time went quickly, and we were soon heading towards our first Christmas.

I didn't know what I wanted to do for that first Christmas, but I knew what I *didn't* want to do. I couldn't face Christmas dinner with those two empty chairs at the table, where Sarah and Vicki would have sat. I couldn't have coped with that.

Our friends Chris and Jeff invited us round to their home for Christmas Day, because the empty chairs wouldn't be so obvious there. And they were right. There will always be two empty chairs where the girls should be, in my life, not just at the dinner table. But the first Christmas was always going to be the hardest.

Christmas Day 1989 fell on a Monday. Trevor was due to finish work on the Friday before Christmas, and on the Thursday I asked my brother to drive me to the local garden centre to buy a Christmas tree. He said, 'I thought you weren't going to have a tree this year,' and I told him I'd changed my mind. So we drove to the garden centre, chose a big tree, a real one like we always had, and brought it home. I asked David to go up into the loft and bring all the Christmas decorations down. My thinking was, the girls would be sad if we didn't have a tree, and so I decided to decorate it in exactly the same way as they had always done. The girls would always decorate the tree with big red velvet bows and baubles and lights, tinsel everywhere. And always the angel on the top.

David and I spent a couple of hours decorating this huge tree. It looked beautiful, and we were really pleased with it. I hadn't planned to do it, but it felt like the right thing.

When Trevor arrived home the following day, I couldn't wait to show him the tree. But he absolutely hated it, telling me to take it down. And he went straight upstairs and got into bed, even though it was the middle of the afternoon. I was so disappointed, because I thought I'd made an effort. I said to him, 'The girls would love it. It's about the girls.'

Trevor was still in bed when it was time to eat. I sent David out to get fish and chips, and when he got home, I went upstairs to Trevor and told him to pull himself together and come downstairs.

'This is as hard for me as it is for you. I'm making an effort, and I expect you to do so too.'

I wasn't going to put up with him coming home and staying in bed for the whole of Christmas. It seemed to me that if that was what he wanted to do, he might as well have stayed with his friends in Dudley.

On Christmas Eve, Trevor and I drove up to Liverpool to lay flowers on the girls' grave and light candles in the cathedral. It became something we would do every year, even after we split up and were divorced: on Christmas Eve, and on each of the girls' birthdays. Vicki's birthday was just after mine in July, and her sixteenth birthday had fallen three months after the disaster, on 20 July.

Sarah's twentieth birthday was on 10 April, so the following year it fell just before the first anniversary. On her last birthday before she died, we had opened a bottle of Moët & Chandon. Sarah really liked that champagne and it became a tradition; on each anniversary since, we've always had a glass to celebrate her birthday together. Trevor was the one person I could share memories of the girls growing up with: their first steps, starting school, their arguments and their unshakeable bond as two teenage sisters growing up.

Chapter 22

LFC and Liverpool City Council had planned a first-anniversary service at Anfield, with input from the committee of the HFSG. It fell on Easter Sunday 1990.

The day before the anniversary, at the match at Anfield, half a dozen bereaved mums, including myself, went onto the pitch at half-time and released a red balloon for each victim of the disaster to enormous applause from the crowd. We were staying in a hotel locally, and we arrived at Anfield early on the Sunday morning to help with the preparations for the service.

There was a podium at the centre of the pitch, where later that day the Bishop of Liverpool and various other clergy would be conducting the service. A red rose, for each person who had died, was going to be given to each of the families at the end of the service, and these had to be laid out on the podium. I was asked if I would wrap foil round the stems of the roses, and so Sean Richardson, a friend of Sarah's, and myself went to the referee's room to perform this task. We noticed that they were long-stemmed red roses, and each of them had a lot of sharp thorns. We kept pricking our fingers, and I said to Sean, 'We need to remove every thorn so none of the families hurt themselves.' So we carefully removed every thorn before we wrapped the stems in the foil.

The families were due to arrive for lunch, and there were so many families that it took up two large rooms at Anfield. The club served a sit-down lunch, and then we all went and sat in the main stand for the service. It was all televised live on the BBC. There was a minute's silence at 3.06 p.m., the time the game was stopped. Even to this day, the whole city stops to remember the victims at 3.06 p.m. on 15 April.

The memorial service was then run by HFSG every year until the thirtieth anniversary, which had to be postponed for legal reasons, and then two years of lockdowns. LFC opened up the Kop every year for the families and the fans to remember. The bells of the city always ring out ninety-six times, in remembrance of the ninety-six.

This all felt completely surreal to me, or as normal as anything had been from that fateful day. I have a 'public mode', an emotionally detached version of myself. It's the way I cope with it all. I don't grieve publicly, and we'd been in the eye of the public constantly for a year by the time of the first anniversary. I always try to be as dignified as I possibly can, as I'm there to represent my daughters. I am still on this journey, still learning to live with my new reality. Every day has become a new learning day.

The following months we went back to the same routine: Trevor in Dudley during the week; me back at work. Life was just trundling along. Or what had become our lives: we were trying to move the justice side of the campaign forwards, there were TV interviews for Trevor and some-times magazine interviews for me.

But as the year wore on, it became increasingly clear to me that Trevor and I were growing apart. I don't know how it had got to this point. Trevor wasn't there most of the time anyway. His role hadn't really changed: he was still the MD of a company, the chair of the HFSG. But he was making no more effort to spend time at home. The only time we spent together was driving in the car up and down to Liverpool. And when we got to the HFSG meetings, he was up with the committee and I was part of the audience. What was I supposed to do? I'd lost my role in life, as a mum. I felt redundant – I needed to find a new role. I needed space to find out who I was. I had to find me again.

I guess, with Trevor working away in a different part of the country, leaving me in London, our relationship didn't stand much of a chance of surviving. Not a snowball's chance in hell. However, people are naturally curious and, even now, complete strangers will ask me if we split up because of the disaster. Everyone wants a black-and-white answer. But is life ever as simple as that? When you look at the figures, 70 per cent of people are said to break up after the death of a child and, in our case, we had become childless.

There are many reasons why a marriage might fail after a tragedy, as we all deal with grief in different ways. In our case, we had become childless and would never be grandparents. Perhaps if we had been able to spend more time together, things would have turned out differently. However, I do think that if the girls had still been alive, or indeed if one of them had survived, I would not have initiated the split with Trevor in the way that I did, had we not gone to that fateful football match.

When we accepted we were going to separate, I wanted to be near to my girls so that I could visit them more easily, so I looked for a house near to the Woolton and Allerton area of Liverpool, while Trevor looked to move back up to North Yorkshire where he had been offered another job. Trevor's firm decided to buy the house from us, so it was all very straightforward without the usual fees, chains and other dilemmas that can occur.

Trevor didn't seem too happy about me leaving him, which surprised me. But then I thought maybe it was because I had taken control of the situation, when in his work he was always in control. We started divorce proceedings far too soon after the split, as I had no idea about the divorce process, and was not at all sensible about things like maintenance and pensions or anything financial. I wasn't interested in money. I was not in a fit state to even think about it, and just couldn't have cared less. I was what you might call a fool to myself.

When I told my brother David that Trevor and I were splitting up, and told him the details, he was horrified. A couple of days later, he came down and took me to dinner for a brotherly chat. He said to me, 'You've lost the girls, and now you're throwing the rest of it away.' Basically, he wanted to try to knock some sense into my head.

We'd agreed a fifty/fifty split, which was legally correct, as the house was owned jointly in both our names – everything was. I counted all the cutlery up and equally divided all the knives, forks and spoons.

'One for Trevor, one for me, one for Trevor, one for me . . .'

Teacups. Plates, saucers, dinner services all split in two. Even the girls' possessions. Their clothes and books. If there was anything we both wanted, we'd throw a dice to see who got it. I thought to myself, *What have we come to?* The only thing I was dishonest about were two books on Sarah's shelf, *Animal Farm* and *To Kill a Mockingbird,* which she'd asked me to read but I had never got round to it. So I decided I wasn't going to let Trevor have them, as the books were between Sarah and me, so I hid them.

After twenty-four years of marriage, I ended up with very little. I bet Trevor's lawyers must have been laughing their heads off at me.

How was I supposed to make rational decisions about money, my future and things like that when I was living on a day-to-day, sometimes moment-to-moment basis? I wasn't capable at that time of making any sensible decisions about my future. Who would be? I would like to think I would be a lot more sensible now and not so naive. But that is only with hindsight; I really don't think I could have been any different. And even though Trevor was financially better off after the divorce, he was in no better state emotionally than I was.

Leaving Trevor in the way that I did, so soon after our daughters were killed, wasn't the most rational or best decision I'd ever made in my life. Nor was it the most sensible. We'd been warned by our social workers not to make any important decisions for at least two years after a massive trauma like ours, yet here I was, leaving Trevor, and moving to live in a new city – running away. My brother was right: I'd lost the girls, and now I was throwing the rest of it away. It has since made me realise there needs to be a lot more discretion in law in cases of divorce after disasters and trauma.

I didn't make the decisions I made at the time to deliberately mess my life up. I foolishly thought I was making the right decisions. The only excuse I have is that I was simply trying to survive.

Chapter 23

During the summer of 1990, Trevor hired a removal van and drove me up to Liverpool. I had bought a little terraced house in a mews that was part of a Grade 2 listed former riding stables in Gateacre village, a lovely suburb of Liverpool not far from Allerton Cemetery. I had made many good friends in Liverpool by this time, some through the HFSG and others who had been so supportive since the disaster, and then of course there was the gang at Liverpool uni. They'd moved out into student houses at the start of the second year, but I still saw them all regularly.

Every Wednesday night Steve would phone and say, 'Right, I'm going to cook curry for you tonight,' and invite me round to his student house. Steve always made great curries; I was so impressed by his culinary skills. But one night I discovered that, behind the scenes, his friend Ruben who came from an Indian heritage and who knew how to make all this wonderful Asian food, was cooking it for Steve to pass off as his own! Steve never missed a trick. How he managed to deal with somebody in the state I was in, I will never know. As I said to Steve's mum, 'You should be so proud of your boy, he has been amazing. I like to think that, if the roles had been reversed, my girls would have helped you in the same way.'

While I felt sadness at splitting up from Trevor, the truth was I wasn't used to having him around anyway. I probably saw Trevor more often now than I had when we were married. He'd been working away for so long, so I'd learned to be responsible for myself and the girls. And now that the girls were just down the road from me in the cemetery and I could visit them as often as I liked, I felt a huge sense of relief and comfort. I was near them again, and that counted for so much. With friends calling round to help me to get the house straight, and on occasion staying overnight, I didn't get a chance to feel lonely – and that suited me.

It was one afternoon in early autumn that I took myself off to the shops in the city centre and brought myself a pair of comfy boots before I started uni myself. With the access course I'd taken in London before I'd moved up, I'd applied to do a degree at Liverpool John Moores University and been accepted. The degree course was in psychology and criminal justice, where I studied under the esteemed Joe Sim, Professor of Criminology and Co-Director of the Centre for the Study of Crime, Criminalisation and Social Exclusion. I loved the course and made a lot of friends, who I regularly socialised with.

Alongside my new friends, I had other groups of friends and individuals who were a great support to me. Through HFSG I met Gill. She was twenty-six when she lost her husband Nick Joynes at Hillsborough, after only six months of marriage. Gill was working as an air stewardess at the time and she introduced me to her air-crew friends, and later as part of a group we would sometimes go on skiing trips together.

I also made lifelong friends with the lovely Hadley family. Ralph Hadley was a Liverpool fan and at Hillsborough on the day with his best friend, who was killed in the crush. In the aftermath, Ralph vowed to attend all the funerals of those who had died, but after watching Vicki and Sarah's internment he was so upset, he could not attend any others. I stayed with Ralph and his wife Marie and their children in Christmas 2019; they too are very special to me, as is Barbara in St Helens. I first met Barbara and her husband Graham on the day of the girls' funeral, when she put on the tea after the girls' burial. Barbara became my closest confidante at this time, and even gave me a key to her house where I had a room. She never judged me but listened endlessly as I laughed, cried, despaired and got angry. I was visiting the girls' grave every Sunday at midday, regular as clock-work, and every time I got home there was a message on my answering machine, inviting me for a Sunday roast at Barbara's. She was and is always there for me, as is Norma and her husband Mike, and of course Mark and Steve at Liverpool uni. I was so fortunate to have these people in my life then, and I will always be grateful to them for helping me to survive.

That first year I was in Liverpool, my house was never empty. I had two student lodgers living with me, and we had a proper student house going, with a rota for cooking and cleaning. But when we went out, I regressed to being eighteen years old again, and was out clubbing in the evenings with my friends at John Moores or Sarah's friends at Liverpool uni. I'd never been to uni, so it was all new to me. As Steve said, 'We treated Jenni like she was the same age as us. Not like we were taking our mum out with us. She became part of every coming together, every break-up, the boys' arguments with the girls, the girls' arguments with the boys. She became part of that gang. And I think, naively, we did the best thing that we could have done by not applying any filters to it at all. We were subjecting a woman in her early forties to an environment that one should not really revisit at that age, because it's just a bunch of kids off their heads doing what kids do. There was no particular planning, we were just enjoying ourselves.'

I'd become two people. The real me was still Sarah and Vicki's mum, and that serious side came out whenever I had to do anything to do with the Hillsborough disaster. I wore different clothes and was a different person.

But the other me, the student Jenni, loved going out. I had two students living with me for six months, and I loved that I didn't have to think and could be someone else. It was pure escapism, from the pain and fight for truth and justice for the girls.

I had gone from this mum with a family where everything had to be planned to the letter to a person with no family and a no-consequences attitude. But the way I see it, if Sarah hadn't met Mark and Steve and her other friends at uni, I don't know where I would have been. I don't think I would have even survived that first summer. They were my inheritance from Sarah.

Ironically, I hadn't smoked in all the time the girls were alive, not since I had found out I was pregnant with Sarah. But soon I was smoking regularly again. I sometimes think how strange the girls would have found it to see their mum with a cigarette, out clubbing with Sarah's friends. I also started to get a taste for the classic student drinks, especially Beck's lager. One day I was reading a magazine and saw an interview Trevor had given. He said, 'My wife only ever used to drink a glass of wine but now that she's out there with the students, she drinks Beck's from the bottle.'

What a lovely description of me! But at that time, it summed me up perfectly, because that is exactly what I was doing: I was going clubbing in Liverpool where Sarah used to go to with her friends. I look back now and think, *Who was that woman?*

While I had been trying to find myself since the split with Trevor, just twelve weeks after I moved to Liverpool, Trevor had already found someone new. He didn't make me aware of this until after the divorce was finalised, but I was surprised at how quickly I had been replaced. Later I met her and found she was a lovely girl who was friendly and kind. Although she was several years younger than Trevor, she had an understanding about the things Trevor and I still needed to do on behalf of our daughters. He still needed to come over to go to the cemetery on the girls' birthdays, and we shared our flowers and had lunch together on those days. I would see him at the HFSG meetings and we would talk. Sometimes she would come along too.

I think in my head I still believed that at some point Sarah and Vicki were going to come home and walk through the door. And I half expected that, if I went around a corner, I would see them coming the other way. I would be driving along when the dark reality of what had happened would raise its head. It might be a song that triggered it, or a smell, and I'd think '*but Sarah and Vicki are*—' and I don't even now like saying the word 'dead', but I'd have to admit it to myself. And now, over thirty years later, it still takes my breath away, and I still don't know how I have managed to live with their loss.

During that October, actions were brought against South Yorkshire Police. The force admitted it was negligent, had failed in its duty of care to the victims and promptly settled the claims. Of course, you can *never* ever compensate for the loss of a child or a parent or spouse, but it seemed ludicrous to me that even though SYP had admitted they were culpable in a civil court, only two months earlier the CPS had said there wasn't enough evidence to prosecute. It just beggared belief. The families had gaping wounds, and it was keeping them open. I would later learn that what is said in a civil court doesn't stand up in a criminal one, but even this early on in proceedings, I realised that the legal system was not fit for purpose. And with the main inquest looming, there were even more shocks in store.

Chapter 24

In November 1990, a year and seven months since my girls died, the inquest into the Hillsborough disaster under coroner Dr Stefan Popper began and, like many of the victims' families, I made the long trek over from Liverpool to Sheffield as often as I could. Expecting to hear the truth of how my girls had died, I was horrified as I sat there in the courtroom, alongside the other family members and listened to the police making statement after statement about drunk and ticketless Liverpool fans arriving late being to blame for the disaster. It was as if the Taylor Inquiry didn't exist! And early on it became obvious to me and the other families attending that the police statements had been changed, as they sounded all the same, almost as if they were adhering to some kind of script – just too pat. While a few others were plainly ridiculous, including mention of fans carrying carafes of wine at the match. Who carries a carafe of wine at a match? Cans, maybe.

Then came the story, given in evidence in open court, that had made me sick to my stomach when I first read it in the *Sun* all those months ago, of an officer struggling to lift a young lifeless girl out of the crush as fans shouted lewdly, 'Throw her up here and we will f★★★ her.' The girl the *Sun* had 'thought' to be the youngest of the Hicks sisters.

When I heard this, the same thought went through my mind as when I'd seen it in the *Sun* a few days after the disaster. The police couldn't hear people in the pens crying out for help, yet this officer reckoned he'd heard that. I'd like to know how.

I was disgusted and felt betrayed. It took all my strength not to shout out at the injustice of it all. If there had been any doubt before, there was none now. The police were victim-blaming to exonerate themselves. It was the stitch-up that Trevor and I had feared from the outset. That grieving families would have to sit and listen to the police blatantly smearing the fans and their loved ones with their lies, including schoolchildren like the youngest boy, Jon-Paul Gilhooley, aged ten, and Vicki, the youngest girl at fifteen – it was despicable. What it also made me realise was that this was why Graham McCombie hadn't been able to look me in the eye at the mini-inquests. He must have picked up what was going on behind the scenes with the West Midlands force 'investigating' their chums in the South Yorkshire Police and known what was coming. I don't believe for one minute he would have liked this; Graham was a decent man.

As we listened to the statements, it also became clear that the South Yorkshire Police and the pathologists were setting up the story that the victims would all have been dead in seconds: they claimed that 'traumatic asphyxia' was the cause of death in all cases. They claimed that nobody suffered, nobody would have been aware there were any problems. I never believed that for a moment, not from the evidence we'd already heard, and not least with Sarah still

being warm much later than this, but the coroner refused
to hear any evidence of life after 3.15. His reasoning being
that people were already dead and beyond saving by then.
This reasoning still beggars belief, because for every single
one of the victims to have died in that stadium at exactly
the same time that day would have meant a bomb had
gone off or an explosion of some kind. No, the coroner,
to my mind, was covering up for the emergency services
by implying it would have been no use calling in the other
ambulances that were standing idly by because everyone
was already dead by then. He was also covering for the
police, who would not let them through. We could only
hope the jury had the sense to see through these lies and
bogus statements.

During the coffee break one morning, I was standing in the
queue when I glimpsed someone behind me and realised it
was the match commander on the day, Chief Superintendent
David Duckenfield, in full uniform and braids. How arrogant
and insensitive of him to stand behind me like that at the
inquest. Theresa Glover, who had lost her twenty-year-old
son Ian in the disaster yelled at him, 'What are you doing
in uniform, Mr Duckenfield? You're suspended!'

But the police were using every trick in the book to
make themselves look good.

Once the inquest had begun, I was going up to Sheffield
at least two days a week on my study days off from college,
and with my course work and all the travelling, getting up
at 5 a.m. every morning and not getting home until eight
at night, was tiring. From January 1991, all of the major
players in the disaster (such as David Duckenfield, Bernard

Murray, Roger Greenwood, etc.) were due to give their evidence. It was clear I would need to spend a lot more time at the inquest, and so I asked my tutor if I could have more time off, maybe even take a sabbatical until the end of the inquest. He had no idea what I was talking about. I had so successfully separated the two sides of my life, he didn't even know I'd lost my daughters or I had anything to do with Hillsborough.

'You mean to tell me you've been doing all your course work and lectures and going to your daughters' inquests at the same time?'

I told him I had. He suggested I should take the whole year off and come back and restart my degree course the following academic year. He was only trying to be helpful, and he was probably right. But I was determined to complete the year, so I took off from January to the end of the inquest, which finished shortly before Easter. I then went back for the summer term. I was so emotionally and physically drained by the inquest – and so for the last month of it, I managed to stay up in Sheffield in the week. I found a hotel that would give me a reduced rate, which included breakfast and an evening meal. So after court each day, I would go back to the hotel and have a proper meal which kept my strength up and made a huge difference to getting through each day.

Four months on, at the end of March 1991, the jury came in and returned a majority verdict of accidental death. There was shock and outrage in the court. People were crying, people were rushing out upset and others were shouting, 'Cover-up! It's a bloody cover-up!'

I sat in stunned silence amid the pandemonium all around me. It was indeed a cover-up. Trevor, ever the voice of reason, called for calm and another meeting, while former teacher Veronica McAllister, who'd lost her son Francis at Hillsborough, got to her feet and began singing 'You'll Never Walk Alone'. Veronica was the kindest, loveliest lady and a Catholic, who used to hold little masses for us all. But there was to be no justice here, so I got to my feet and joined in with the singing.

To this day, I truly believe that when Margaret Thatcher and Douglas Hurd, who was Home Secretary at the time, went up to Hillsborough on the Sunday after the disaster, that's when this cover-up was first set in motion. I am convinced it was Thatcher's thank you to Peter Wright, the Chief Constable of SYP, for crushing the miners who were picketing at Orgreave Colliery, Rotherham during the NUM strike against pit closures. Many of the police, including those on horseback, had brutally charged at the miners with batons, causing several of them to suffer broken bones and other serious injuries. But to shift blame from themselves onto the victims, Wright ensured that the police statements were dictated and altered in parts to suit their narrative. They used the same methods with us at Hillsborough, even using some of the same officers, and got away with it for decades.

In return, I believe Thatcher then backed the police up at Hillsborough and turned a blind eye to the fate of our loved ones who were crushed to death and seriously injured. This is just my opinion. I haven't got evidence for this, though much later the Hillsborough

Independent Panel (HIP) would look for it. But of course there wouldn't be any evidence – it would all have been shredded long ago. But to me, for Hillsborough to have lasted this length of time, and with the HIP evidence we now have, this wasn't about a handful of officers, because it simply could not have got this far without authority from the very top.

After the inquest, I threw myself back into my uni work, and I managed to just about scrape through the year with a pass. I'll never know how I did that. By the summer it was clear I needed to get away from it all.

One day I was thumbing through an old address book and stumbled on one of my old neighbours from Thornaby, Norma, who was Sarah's godmother. I hadn't spoken to Norma and her husband in years, but I knew they'd emigrated to Canada. So, I telephoned her in Canada and we chatted and I told her what had happened. She knew all about the girls, as the story had been covered on the TV news in Canada, and she was very sorry but she hadn't known how to contact me. She remarked, 'You must come over here sometime,' and of course I politely replied that I'd love to. The moment I got off the phone I rang the travel agent and booked a flight for the next day. Then I rang Norma straight back.

'I've booked it. I'm coming over with Air Canada from Manchester tomorrow!'

I didn't really give her any choice! How could she say no?

This is how I lived through those years: nothing was planned, everything was done on a whim. If I thought something might make me feel better, I just did it. I didn't think anything through, consequences didn't exist, because I couldn't think further than the moment I was in – not even the day, but the moment.

It was so lovely to see Norma again, a happy friendly face from my past, and she and her husband took me to places like Toronto and the glorious Niagara Falls, but all the while I kept thinking how my girls would have loved it here. They were constantly on my mind.

With lots of friends still around, life was hectic and full-on. But it was also becoming more serious too. I was still a very active member of the HFSG, which meant seeing Trevor regularly while the divorce was going through. I hadn't gone back to uni for my second year, and I started to focus on getting my house in order. I'd been using it as a place to sleep; now it was time to make it into a proper home. And when a place on the HFSG committee came up in late 1992, I was proposed and voted on.

I had begun growing up for the second time in my life, even before Mark and Steve and my other student friends had left university in Liverpool to start new jobs and get married and have families.

After they had all graduated and left Liverpool, I applied for and got a job at Barclays Bank, before moving on to the Royal Insurance company as I tried to make a new life for myself. I had to get a job and I had to hold it down as I had no other income or means of support – I needed to earn money to keep a roof over my head. The routine was important in moving my life forward. I enjoyed both those jobs; they gave me a sense of responsibility and I formed new friendships there. Also, I was genuinely surprised and pleased by how much the companies I worked for valued the work I was doing. It began to increase my confidence. But my emotions were still all over the place and I was far more vulnerable than I thought I was, as I would soon find out.

During the late autumn of 1993, after tireless campaigning, an application was made to have the inquest verdicts quashed using the cases of six representative victims' families. The HFSG wasn't formally part of the case, but I went down to London and stayed with my brother for the duration of the case, and attended court every day to support Doreen and Les and the others.

This judicial review included Anne Williams' evidence obtained from officers who had attempted to resuscitate her fifteen-year-old son Kevin and said that he'd uttered 'Mum' at 4 p.m., a long time after the 3.15 cut-off point. And evidence that statements by the officers were later changed following visits from the West Midlands Police, the investigating force into Hillsborough, to suggest there were no signs of life after 3.15 p.m.

Despite this, Lord Justice McCowan, in his wisdom, said he 'could see no fault in the coroner' cutting off the scope of the inquests at 3.15 p.m. because he had relied on medical evidence, and so he refused the application to have the verdicts overturned. This was another blow, although once again it covered very nicely for the emergency services' lack of response, despite the forty-four ambulances and eighty-plus staff that could have helped the victims that day. We all left the court feeling demoralised. It would be yet another Christmas without justice for the victims and their families. Another year without healing.

Chapter 25

I had settled on the committee of the HFSG by now. Trevor was still chair, which could have been difficult because of the tough stance he had taken on the divorce settlement, but we managed to put this aside at meetings and worked well together in a professional capacity.

After the farce of the first inquests, Chief Superintendent David Duckenfield was due to face police disciplinary action for his (mis)handling of events at Hillsborough and as a group, we waited to see how this would go. But before the action could even start, Duckenfield was retired on medical grounds with depression and post-traumatic stress disorder (PTSD) and the action was dead in the water. As far as I could see this saved the face of South Yorkshire Police who would not now come under any further public scrutiny via the match commander, while Duckenfield said his goodbyes on a full police pension plus a golden handshake. In the New Year, charges against Superintendent Bernard Murray, the police control box commander on the day, were also dropped as it was deemed unfair for him to continue to face disciplinary procedures when Duckenfield would not. And so both men walked away without any accountability whatsoever.

As might be expected with all the families, on hearing this news I was very down, albeit no longer surprised at the way things were going. The optimism I had felt following the Taylor Inquiry now seemed like a very long time ago, and I guess I was not really thinking straight when the following year I agreed to let my ex-husband into my life again.

Possibly because I didn't really fight Trevor over financial matters during the break-up, it enabled us to have a more amicable relationship. As well as his work with HFSG, Trevor now owned his own company, so he was riding high at that point. The little contact we still had with each other, aside from at the group, was when we would visit our daughters' graves together. He also sent me flowers every Mother's Day from the girls, to help me get through that day, so we had a reasonably amicable relationship. We are joint executors of the girls' estates too, and with the paperwork still to sort out at the time, Trevor asked me if he could come over one Sunday to go through it.

'Of course,' I said, 'and I'll cook us lunch.'

I sorted out lunch before Trevor arrived, then we went to the cemetery while the food was cooking. After putting our flowers on the grave, we stayed and talked about the girls for a while, remembering them together. These shared memories are so very important to me. Then we came back, had the meal and went through all the girls' paperwork. When we finished around seven in the evening, as Trevor was about to leave, he pulled me to him and said, 'I feel like a lovesick schoolboy over you.'

It was both bizarre and unexpected. 'Oh, stop it, Trevor!' I said, thinking he was joking.

But he replied, 'No, I'm serious.' And then he left to go back home to his fiancée in North Yorkshire.

I didn't take him seriously, but soon after, I started to get phone messages from Trevor left on my answering machine and find notes pushed through my door when I came home from work. And one Saturday he turned up in the car and sat outside my house while I was at work. When he realised I wasn't there, he went round to my friend Doreen's house to see if I was there. On Valentine's Day he sent me Valentine's cards and flowers and told me he was still in love with me. I was apprehensive about all this, but he began to revive all the feelings I'd had for him when we first got together. While it confused me, it also gave me comfort, and perhaps it did for Trevor too. We started going on dates, and I found myself sleeping with him again and turning into my ex-husband's 'other woman'. The only problem was I really liked his fiancée, and I felt guilty at having an affair with Trevor behind her back. But Trevor convinced me he wasn't just fooling around. He wanted me to move in with him and for us to get remarried.

I was so confused, but after a while I started to quite like the idea, and I found comfort in the idea of going back to what I knew. Even though I had a good job now and friends who I regularly went out to dinner with, or to the cinema, I was still just living my life day-to-day.

After a couple of months, he told me he was selling his cottage and had bought a converted barn and was renovating it. He even brought the plans round and wanted me to help. But his fiancée and he moved into the barn a few months later, which I thought was odd. If there was ever a time to tell her about us, it was then.

Leading up to Vicki's twenty-first birthday, Trevor suggested we should go out and have a really special day together.

Vicki's birthday was in July and with Trevor planning a surprise for me, I asked the Royal Insurance company if I could take the day off. I explained it was for Vicki's twenty-first and they were very understanding and agreed. The day before Vicki's birthday, as I was leaving for work, the phone rang. It was Trevor, telling me quite matter-of-factly that there was change of plan for tomorrow.

'OK, Trevor. What's the change of plan then?' I asked him, looking forward to us spending time together on Vicki's birthday.

He told me his fiancée would now be coming with him.

His fiancée was coming with him? I went over that in my head so many times. His fiancée was coming with him? *How's that going to work?* Had I gone mad, or had he? Here I was, having an affair with Trevor, and he was bringing his fiancée with us to celebrate our youngest daughter's twenty-first birthday.

He told me that the reason she was coming was because he was buying her a palomino pony from a stable near Haydock, which they had to pass on the way to Liverpool.

But why was he buying her a palomino pony when he had suggested we move in together and remarry? I didn't know what he was talking about. I was even more confused. I obviously didn't know the rules of having an affair.

His suggestion was he would drop his fiancée off in Liverpool city centre to do some shopping, then come round to take me to the cemetery, and then he would pick her up afterwards. So much for our special celebration for Vicki's twenty-first birthday. And for our future plans together.

I was astounded. I couldn't even answer him. I put the phone down. None of it made sense. I felt devastated. It was like the previous six months had never happened. Selling me the false idea that we would have another life together, and then taking it away. Could he not at least have waited until after our daughter's birthday?

However, people don't always behave how we expect or like them to. We were two damaged people, trying to find some comfort. The numbness that had surrounded the loss and devastation was wearing off, and reality was setting in.

I knew I couldn't go into work that day, so I telephoned my friend Doreen. It was while I was speaking to her that the tears came.

The next day, on Vicki's birthday, Doreen and I went to the Anglican Cathedral and lit candles. Then we went to the cemetery to take the flowers I had bought. As we reached the girls' graves, I sank to my knees and began shouting at Doreen, 'Why are my daughters down that hole? Why are they down that f★★★ing hole?'

I knew I was frightening Doreen, but I couldn't stop it. I had no control over what I was doing. And I felt terrible about it. Eventually, after some time, I must have worn myself out as I found myself lying on the grass near the grave. I wanted to stay there forever. Doreen had been so supportive but I just couldn't stop.

Eventually, Doreen persuaded me I'd feel better if I went back to her house and had a cup of tea, and she rang my friend Barbara in St Helens and told her I wasn't well. Barbara came and picked me up, and I stayed at her house for over a week. I was vulnerable, and emotionally exhausted, and she looked after me and let me sleep and talk about anything. I could just be me with her.

A week after Vicki's birthday, I knew I would be seeing Trevor at a family support group meeting the following Sunday. So I decided I would ask him to come back to my house in Gateacre after the meeting and explain what the affair had been all about.

I thought this might help me get my head round what had gone wrong, and Trevor agreed. I can remember him standing at one side of my kitchen and me at the other as I said, 'Trevor I don't – I can't – get my head round what is happening.'

He told me coldly that he had decided that he thought the world of his fiancée. That was the only explanation he ever gave me. He had no reason other than that he had simply changed his mind. Yet, he'd seemed so genuine, and it had taken him a long time to convince me that moving in with him and his marriage proposal were a good idea. He inferred I'd taken it all a bit too seriously.

One of the recurring nightmares I was having at the time involved me being back in the North Stand at Hillsborough, seeing all these poor people lying on the pitch injured and dying, and others desperately trying to help them. I don't think I'd ever acknowledged all this before. I'd been blocking it out, in denial, and those scenes were a living nightmare. The only problem was, when I woke up, I would find it was still going on in my room. I could physically see the pitch and the people there dying and the fans screaming. All that I had witnessed on that April day was suddenly right there in front of me. I had several months of this abject hell, but once again I was so blessed to have had the right people in my life at the time: good friends like Barbara and Doreen and my GP, who I would go to see every Monday morning. She would say, 'Don't worry about appointments, I will fit you in whenever you turn up.'

She was so kind. I would see her every Monday as she tried to help me with the emotional pain I was in, and for the nightmares which were so bad at this time, I thought I was losing my mind. After a while I began to see her on Thursday afternoons for aromatherapy sessions. I went to meditation sessions too, where the lady taking them would stand behind me and say, 'You're going down some steps into a beautiful garden . . .' and she would get me to describe it. I found it really relaxing, and I would say to her, 'Wow, I can see all these colours swirling around.' She was an older lady and at the end of each session, she'd say in this amazing throaty voice of hers, 'Now that you are in this garden and you can see all these beautiful roses and smell their fragrance, I want you to pick a rose. What colour is the rose?'

'Purple,' I said.

'Purple is the colour of healing,' she replied.

I still try to visualise purple in my third eye whenever I have a difficult day.

My sessions with my GP for PTSD went on for over two years. Although she helped me through a very difficult time, it would be a long while before I was on the road to recovery. I was still having panic attacks. I didn't understand what they were at first, but they were so frightening. I would feel I couldn't breathe and, as I gasped for breath, I was certain I was having a heart attack and about to die. When it happened in public it was embarrassing and it sapped my confidence, as I'd feel that I wasn't trying hard enough, that I wasn't in control. If I had broken my leg, I could just have been open about it. But with every panic attack I felt that it was my fault, and that I had to pretend I wasn't having one, which only made it worse. I was in such a bad way that my GP referred me to the Alder Centre at the Alder Hey Children's Hospital for Grief and Bereavement Counselling for the loss of a child. On their website it says that the loss of a child is one of the worst things that can happen to a person and that no one experiences loss and grief the same: 'Many feelings may be so mixed up that you wonder if you are going mad or will ever be able to enjoy life again. This is a perfectly normal reaction to the range of emotions involved.'

This alone was an enormous help. I was a mess and I'd probably acted rashly at times, not least with my young student friends, but the Centre seemed to be saying it was OK and that I was OK, and they seemed to understand how I felt. But having lost both my children, I didn't expect too much from the Centre or the counselling, to be honest. However, the Centre was run by a very special lady called Valerie Mandelson, and my goodness did she help me through the trauma of the loss I had suffered. She and the other staff there were amazing.

It was then explained to me about 'powerlessness', where you are forced to stand and witness a traumatic event and there is nothing you can do, you are stuck there just seeing it. It helped me to put a name to what I'd gone through.

I had counselling at the Centre for two years, and that led onto me volunteering at the Centre. I learned so much from having the counselling there, I wanted to give something back. To help other families who found themselves devastated by the loss of a child.

The Alder Centre had set up a Child Death Helpline, coincidentally in 1989, but nothing to do with the Hillsborough disaster. It existed to enable bereaved parents to telephone and talk to someone who understood what they were going through.

We worked on a rota, a couple of nights a week until 10 p.m. at night, and I always offered to do as many shifts as I could. None of us were trained counsellors; we were just people who were there to listen. Our training was clear: we were there to be 'listening ears'. To give the callers an opportunity to unload their feelings, not to intervene.

When you're part of a group of people from the same disaster, as I was in HFSG, you are all facing the same trauma and injustices, the same grief and problems. So working on the helpline opened up a whole new world of child bereavement to me.

The helpline at Alder Hey was seminal. It became so successful that Great Ormond Street Children's Hospital in London decided they wanted to run a similar scheme for bereaved parents, and from there it grew into a National Helpline. And I think it was a two-way process: it helped the parents calling in and it helped me. It was all part of the journey of losing a child or children. 'Journey' is for sure an overused word, but nonetheless it's true – it is a journey, and I volunteered at the helpline for three years and I was privileged to have done so.

Soon I was to receive other news that would set the wheels in motion to make a massive difference to me, and to all the victims' families, as we were presented with an opportunity to shine a beacon of light on the truth.

Chapter 26

In 1995, after five long years of fighting for truth and justice with the other families affected, Doreen and I wrote a letter to the acclaimed TV scriptwriter Jimmy McGovern at Granada TV studios in Manchester, which would eventually start the ball rolling to help get the truth out there on a national level.

Jimmy, a Liverpudlian by birth and an LFC supporter, had created and written the iconic *Cracker* series about a criminal psychologist, which was networked on ITV in the nineties. While Doreen and I recognised Jimmy as a great writer, the letter was actually to complain about a story he'd written featuring a fictitious Hillsborough survivor. However, when Jimmy replied to us, he made the mistake of putting his address on the letter. So Doreen and I came up with a plan to speak to him about doing a programme on Hillsborough. Borrowing Doreen's daughter's dog, we turned up at his house which 'we just happened to be passing' while taking the dog out for a walk. It must have sounded a lot less convincing than we'd anticipated as when we arrived at his address, we found it was in a cul-de-sac!

It was a lovely day and he invited us to share a bottle of wine with him in his garden where we told him our stories, and pleaded, 'You have you got to write something about this, Jimmy! You've got to!'

By the time we'd finished the bottle – or was it two – it was evening, and the dog walked me and Doreen home!

Doreen and I didn't know what would come of it, or if indeed anything would, but I was delighted when I received a phone call from Jimmy.

'Jenni,' he said, 'can I come round to your house to interview you for a programme I want to make about Hillsborough? It will only take a couple of hours.'

He turned up at ten o'clock in the morning and didn't leave until seven that night. He explained the idea he had in mind for the programme. It would be a dramatised documentary about the families who lost loved ones at Hillsborough that day, showing the police cover-up that led up to the first inquest in 1991. This was seminal; no one had done anything like it before, and Doreen and I were so excited when he told us.

But first Jimmy had to speak to the Andrea Wonfor, the then chief executive of Granada TV. Jimmy had won BAFTAs galore for *Cracker* and Andrea, who was on her third large brandy by the time he spoke to her, said, 'Tell me what you need, Jimmy, and you will have it. Now go and do it.'

Andrea had vision and I was so thrilled when Jimmy got the green light. It was the first step to the victims' families being taken seriously, our first step to rebutting the *Sun*'s version of 'the truth', because this was going to be the actual truth.

Eventually the producers decided to focus on three different victims' families to represent the ninety-six. Trevor and I were possibly chosen to be representative of those victims who weren't from Liverpool, and didn't fit the narrative the police and press were trying to portray. I won't pretend it wasn't tough and very emotional going over what happened again for the programme, but it had to be done. We needed to get the truth out there, into the public eye, for the girls, and the other ninety-four victims, and for all the families in our campaign for justice.

It was so important for the HFSG to back this drama. When you begin to realise the iniquitous lies and corruption working against you, and that the government are actually complicit in this, then you do unite together and find a collective strength. Before that match we were just a random group of supporters from different backgrounds, with different life experiences and expectations, but after the tragedy we came together to support each other through our grief, and to fight for truth and justice, and that was powerful. Jimmy's docudrama *Hillsborough* was a breakthrough on that journey for the HFSG and for other families outside the group, as it got the facts out there, which were entirely opposite to what the South Yorkshire Police were saying. As Jimmy himself put it, 'for the first time in a long time for the families, they [the police] were being asked questions set by the drama documentary'. The agenda was the one now set by the programme, which made a refreshing change.

The programme went out the following year, on Thursday, 5 December 1996 in the lead-up to Christmas. On the morning of the screening at BAFTA, Trevor and I were interviewed by Richard and Judy on ITV's *This Morning* in London. Once we'd finished, they had a car ready for us and we were rushed across London to a morning screening at the BAFTA theatre on Piccadilly, arriving halfway through. Originally, I'd said I didn't want to do the Richard and Judy interview. Chris Eccleston, who played Trevor, and Annabelle Apsion, who played me, kindly offered to go on *This Morning* to fill in for us. But the programme makers said that if I didn't go on it with Trevor, they were going to drop the item.

I was so conflicted, but Trevor made the point that it was good publicity, and that was true; they had millions of viewers. I was prepared to do it for the greater good.

The docudrama went out the following night, and the viewing figures for its TV debut were excellent. Jimmy had made a magnificent job of it, and with a great cast, Charles McDougall directing and Katy Jones as factual producer, it was so powerful, so moving and truthful, and in 1997 it went on to win a BAFTA for best single drama, and numerous other awards worldwide.

After the stitch-up of the first inquest, the programme became hugely pivotal in shifting views and moving the discussion on. With the truth emerging at last, it gave me and all the other families somewhere to go legally, and it gave us a sense of purpose. The first seven years after the disaster had been incredibly hard for all of us, but after the docudrama went out, the public's perception of what had happened changed. And on a personal level that lifted my soul and gave me hope that we'd get somewhere now. I know 100 per cent that we'd not be where we are today without Jimmy's *Hillsborough*, and that is why Jimmy will always, always have a special place in my heart.

In April of 1997, on the eighth anniversary of the disaster, Princess Diana sent a message of support to all the families, to be read out at the memorial service at Anfield. It was another important sign that public opinion was turning our way and things were starting to move forward.

My spirits were further raised some five months on from the *Hillsborough* TV premiere, when in May 1997 a new Labour government led by Tony Blair came into power. Jack Straw, when he was shadow Home Secretary, had promised an independent judicial scrutiny of evidence and now he was in office, I thought at last we might get somewhere.

Meanwhile, Trevor, Phil and the HFSG committee were advised to try to bring a private prosecution against those we saw as culpable. Legally, it was our only option. Unfortunately, you cannot do that on legal aid, so we had to find the money for it, a lot of money, and we had to raise it ourselves. People came up with lots of ideas, including charity football matches, then Phil Hammond suggested the best way forward was to hold a fundraising concert at Anfield. We drew up a list of bands and performers to approach and were delighted when some of the best acts in the industry agreed to support us. I think they too were probably influenced by Jimmy's programme. The bands included the Beautiful South, Manic Street Preachers, Lightning Seeds, Stereophonics, Holly Johnson and the Bootleg Beatles, as well as Liverpool bands, Smaller, Space and Dodgy. Also, two gospel choirs: the London Community Gospel Choir and the Love and Joy Gospel Choir. Not a single person involved was paid a fee. It was amazing, but we needed someone to underwrite it in case it all went pear-shaped. Phil and our solicitor Ann Adlington had the idea of approaching Richard Branson, and he agreed to step in, his only concession being that he wanted us to sell only Virgin Cola at the concert, which we were happy to do.

The Hillsborough Justice Concert took place at Anfield on 10 May 1997 and was a huge success – on the day tickets first went on sale, they outsold tickets for the Michael Jackson concert, and it raised almost half a million pounds in total. Phil and Ann Adlington both worked incredibly hard to organise it, and they would go on to work well together for the trial that it paid for.

Shortly after, in June 1997, Jack Straw announced 'scrutiny' of evidence and appointed Lord Justice Stuart-Smith to lead it. However, we weren't aware until years later that Straw didn't believe there was sufficient evidence for a new inquiry. In a civil service note that was later released, he said that any assertion that there was insufficient evidence should come from an independent source such as a judge to be 'acceptable'. And Tony Blair himself had written across the civil service note, 'Why? What is the point' of having another inquiry.

It was no surprise then to find out that this so-called 'scrutiny' was not in fact an inquiry and was limited to only seeing new evidence not already seen by the Taylor Inquiry, the Director of Public Prosecutions (DPP) or any other courts and authorities. So the new evidence that had come out in the judicial review a few years earlier, which had been rejected by Lord Justice McCowan, could not then be heard. This included Ann Williams's evidence.

This scrutiny was a total joke, as became apparent when Lord Justice Stuart-Smith came up to speak to the victims' families in October 1997. No sooner had he stepped foot on Albert Dock in Liverpool to meet them than he quipped to Phil Hammond, vice chair of the HFSG, whose teenage son had died at Hillsborough, that the families of the victims were going to be 'late like the Liverpool supporters on the day'.

Phil Hammond walked away in disgust. It was deeply offensive to the families – if this was the attitude of the judge leading the scrutiny, what chance did it have? But we were legally advised to proceed with Stuart-Smith.

In February 1998 we headed to Westminster to see Jack Straw, and it came as no surprise to us when he said nothing significant had come out of the Stuart-Smith scrutiny to warrant another inquiry. On the day of the announcement South Yorkshire Police held a press conference equipped with flip charts containing extracts of the report, which they had obviously been given in advance. Once again, the Establishment was covering for itself, and this government was no better than the last. New Labour were in office for fifteen years and that was the sum total of all they did for us.

We had no choice but to try and bring private prosecutions against Chief Superintendent David Duckenfield, the match commander, and against Superintendent Bernard Murray, who was the ground controller that day. These commenced in June 1998, and there followed a year of various legal interjections and desperate applications by the defendants' legal teams to have the prosecutions discontinued.

So it was July, 1999, by the time we went to Leeds Magistrates Court. As I sat there alongside some of the other families, all I could think about was what the decision would be. And that was when the stipendiary magistrate, Nigel Cadbury, ruled that the prosecutions could continue to the Crown Court. Finally, it felt like we would have an opportunity to seek justice for our loved ones. I'm not someone who cries in public, but Jimmy McGovern, who'd accompanied me, said he heard someone sobbing and looked all around the room before he realised it was me, sitting right next to him. These were tears of relief that we'd been offered another glimmer of hope.

The wheels of the legal system ground slowly on. It would not be until July 2000 that the cases were heard at Leeds Crown Court in front of Mr Justice Hooper. The families travelled up to Leeds on a coach every day of the trial, which lasted seven weeks. I'd leave home at 6 a.m. and wouldn't get back till after 7 p.m. in the evening. But I didn't miss one day of that trial.

At the conclusion of the evidence, Justice Hooper identified four questions for the jury to consider in turn. If the jury answered the first question 'yes', they were move on to the next. If the jury answered any question 'no', they were to find them not guilty.

Question 1: Was the jury sure that 'by having regard to all the circumstances, it was foreseeable by a reasonable match commander that allowing a large number of spectators to enter the stadium through exit gate C without closing the tunnel would create an obvious and serious risk of death to the spectators in pens 3 and 4?'

Question 2: Could a 'reasonable match commander' have taken 'effective steps . . . to close off the tunnel' thus preventing the deaths?

Question 3: Was the jury sure 'that the failure to take such steps was neglect?'

Question 4: Was the jury sure that the 'failure to take those steps . . . was so bad in all the circumstances as to amount to a very serious criminal offence?'

The jury considered for two days. On the third day, we were called back into the court because the jury had a query about question four. Surely this meant they had answered 'yes' to questions one to three?

We came so close.

At this point, Justice Hooper made his crucial intervention: he noted the 'huge difference between an error of judgement and negligence' and said there were two further key questions:

Would a criminal conviction send out a wrong message to those who have to react to an emergency and take decisions?

Would it be right to punish someone for taking a decision and not considering the consequences in a crisis situation?

I still believe that this was the critical intervention that lost us the case. We are still trying to gain accountability in a criminal court to this day. And there was worse to come.

Murray was cleared of manslaughter, and the jury were unable able to reach a verdict on Duckenfield, who Mr

Justice Hooper ordered should not face a retrial. My tears two years earlier had been wasted. It was a huge disappointment, and I felt that everyone's hard work to raise the money for the prosecutions had been wasted too. But at the same time, it was no surprise, as tight constraints had been placed on these trials right at the start. In particular, no evidence would be heard beyond a 3.06 p.m. cut-off point, which was when the game had been stopped, and seven minutes less than the 3.15 cut-off at the first inquest and at the Stuart-Smith scrutiny. Clearly, it was another stitch-up.

Chapter 27

In the midst of all these legal proceedings, we were approaching the tenth anniversary of Hillsborough, which fell on 15 April 1999.

I decided I was ready to do one of the most difficult things I could ever do: return to Hillsborough. I'd caught the stadium on the news occasionally since the tragedy, but I would always switch off the TV. Psychologists believe it can be cathartic returning to the scene of a deeply traumatic event, but up until that point I had never felt brave enough to do that. But while we were making the docudrama *Hillsborough*, Jimmy McGovern had said to me, 'If you ever feel you want to go back to Hillsborough Stadium, I'll come with you, Jenni.'

I decided to take Jimmy up on that offer. I telephoned him and asked him if he was still up for it, and he was. I telephoned Sheffield Wednesday FC to make the arrangements, and stressed to them, 'I don't want any fuss, and I don't want a welcoming party.'

I certainly didn't want to see Graham Mackrell, who had been safety officer at the time of the disaster and was now Club Secretary.

It was snowing heavily when we got to Lime Street station in Liverpool City Centre, but despite all the snow and ice, the trains were still running. When we arrived at Sheffield, we took a taxi to the ground where there actually was a welcoming party of sorts, including the club's chaplain. I asked, 'What's he doing here?'

'He's come to show you around,' they replied.

It was emotional as we walked out of the player's entrance, onto the track that surrounded the pitch, and headed towards the Leppings Lane end of the ground. So here I was, on an icy cold snowy January day, standing on the very pitch where my daughters had lay dying ten years earlier.

We walked across the pitch and into the goalmouth. Closer and closer to the pens where my daughters had been crushed to death. I asked if I could walk down the tunnel, which had been Sarah and Vicki's last journey alive.

I already knew the pens were no longer there – it was an all-seater open terrace now, very different. This was one of the positive things that had come out of the Taylor Report, following the Hillsborough disaster. I looked over at the North Stand, where I had sat on that April day, and realised just how near to the disaster I had been. So near, and yet unable to do anything to help my daughters.

The chaplain asked if I wanted to go into the gymnasium.

I caught my breath: the gymnasium had of course been the temporary mortuary. But I wasn't going to come all this way and not go into the gymnasium.

When my brother David had called me a few days earlier, I told him I was going to go back to the ground. He'd said, 'You do know the place is haunted, don't you?'

He told me that they had been having all sorts of problems in the club offices, which were next to the gymnasium:

computers turning on and off, lights going on and off, alarms going off in the middle of the night. 'I read it in the *Daily Star*,' he said.

I laughed, and said sarcastically, 'Well it must be true if you read it in a red top, David!'

But a spooky story was nothing compared to seeing Sarah and Vicki lying on the dirty gymnasium floor in those body bags. That had been the very worst moment of my entire life, and had returned to me in flashbacks and nightmares ever since. But today, I had ghosts of my own to lay. I wanted to go back into that place – I needed to – so I steeled myself and we headed towards the gymnasium. When we walked in, there was a feeling of peace I hadn't expected. So I said to the chaplain, 'It is so peaceful in here. Especially as my brother tells me it's haunted.'

I was expecting a denial, but the chaplain told me it was true. He said, 'I had to come and exorcise it with candles and prayers.'

And there was me knocking the *Daily Star*!

'Well, whatever you've done, there is a feeling of peace here now.'

He told me that since the exorcism they hadn't had any more problems.

How fascinating is that? I thought to myself. Jimmy couldn't even open his mouth to say a word.

We were then invited to go for tea and biscuits in the boardroom, but as soon as I got in there, I felt uncomfortable. There was a feeling of unrest, something hostile. I wanted to leave. I said to Jimmy, 'I need to go home now.'

On the train back, I was pleased I had managed to make

this visit. It was another huge step on my journey of facing my demons, while the fight for truth and justice for my girls and for all the victims continued.

By the autumn of 2001 it was clear that it was necessary for me to get back to work. I needed to start earning money again, and I'd always worked. I saw an advertisement for temporary Christmas jobs at a flagship M&S store at a retail park in Warrington and decided I would give it a go.

I've never worked so physically hard in all my life! I was put in the childrenswear department, and you weren't allowed to sit down, apart from a couple of breaks: eight hours straight, in heels. And at Christmas too. After a few days, I wasn't sure I could make it from the store to my car at the end of the day, my feet hurt so much. The next day I went to buy myself some flat shoes. By the end of Christmas I was delighted to say goodbye.

But the following spring, I was surprised to be offered a permanent job back at the same store. It hadn't been my favourite job, but I'd clearly made a good impression! And it was a job, and I had bills to pay.

The thing I liked best about my job at M&S was chatting to the customers and helping them. However, the thing that made it most enjoyable for me was my colleagues. I was working with a great bunch of people, and it was there I started to find a different me.

One particular friend was sixteen-year-old Rachel Lester, who was studying for her A levels at a nearby sixth-form college. She reminded me of Vicki with her beautiful face, large eyes and long dark hair. She also made me laugh, and

I became her 'work mum'. She is another of those special people who have become part of my life since the disaster, and I have remained her second mum ever since. We see each other regularly, and Rachel is one of the most special people in my life.

At M&S I really began to feel that I was laying down positive building blocks for the future. I had been at the job for about two years when the manager called me into his office and I thought, *Oh no! I'm going to be told off for doing something wrong!* I was so nervous when I went in, but to my surprise, the manager said to me, 'I just wanted to let you know that you're an inspiration.'

I thought I'd misheard him. 'An inspiration?' I asked him.

'Yes,' he said, 'you are. We all get bad days and down days, and when I'm having a day where I'm feeling sorry for myself, I think of you.'

I was flabbergasted. Then he said, 'I've seen you speaking on television, and I watch how you are on the shop floor with the customers and with your colleagues, and you really are an inspiration.'

That took me back because, even though it was over ten years since the disaster, I still didn't really know who I was any more. I'd gone out with my daughters one morning to a football match, and I'd come home without them, and without a future. I'd lost my place in the world. But here I was an inspiration to the manager of this large, quality store. I really appreciated his words – they meant such a lot to my self-worth.

I didn't realise how low my self-esteem had become until it started to go up again. Until people started recognising me in my own right, not just as somebody's wife. Even before the tragedy, when I was out working and running the home, I always thought of Trevor as the important one who did all the clever things. He was one of those people who could turn his hand to anything, and he was always very popular, especially with women. He used to say the girls got their brains from him, and their looks from me. The sad thing is, at the time I accepted and was quite happy with that.

However, with the respect that I was now getting from my M&S colleagues at all different levels of management, and the customers too, it made my confidence and self-belief start to grow, and I realised that, after all that had happened, I could be just as capable as anyone else.

Chapter 28

Fifteen years after the girls died, Trevor was planning to remarry so stepped down from his commitment as chair of the Hillsborough Family Support Group. I was pleased that he'd found happiness again, although it was far too much information when he told me he'd found the 'love of his life', and she would become my daughters' step-mother. Especially as we'd been married for twenty-four years and had produced two beautiful children together. But I let the insensitive comments go, to enable me to move forward.

Phil Hammond, who had been vice chair, gave up his managerial job at the Post Office to take over from Trevor as chair. Phil worked tirelessly, something he demonstrated through his work on the Hillsborough concert and private prosecution, working day and night to get them off the ground. Phil was chair for five years, with me as the group's secretary. But as we approached the twentieth year of the disaster, he became unwell and sadly was unable to continue in the role. He had put his heart and soul into the fight for justice and his stepping down as chair was greatly felt. Without Phil, I truly believe the private prosecution in 2000 would not have happened. Phil was then succeeded by Margaret Aspinall, who had lost her teenage son James at Hillsborough, and I was elected as her vice chair, a role that I still hold to this day.

After several long years and decades of campaigning, it began to feel as if things were beginning to look up when, just days before the twentieth anniversary of Hillsborough in April 2009, Maria Eagle, then a junior justice minister in Gordon Brown's Labour government and local MP for Garston and Halewood, accused South Yorkshire Police of a 'black propaganda campaign' to deflect blame from themselves onto the Liverpool supporters. Maria had already asserted this in the House of Commons in May 1998 several weeks after the publication of the Stuart-Smith Scrutiny, but her reasserting it now was the huge boost that we needed.

Then on 15 April 2009, the twentieth anniversary of Hillsborough, Andy Burnham, the then Secretary of State for Culture, Media and Sports, gave a speech at Anfield for the memorial service and mentioned the injustice. He was interrupted by a lone voice from the Kop shouting out, 'You've got to do something about it, Andy!'

Then, the rest of the Kop backed him up, singing 'Justice for the ninety-six, justice for the ninety-six!'

The following day, Andy and Maria called on the government for all of the Hillsborough documentation to be released early, rather than under the usual thirty-year ruling. The Rt Hon Michael Wills and PM Gordon Brown supported their call for disclosure, and it was agreed that an independent inquiry which focused entirely on the documentation should be set up. Without their support this would not have been achieved. The HFSG had set up an executive committee to assist with this, chaired by Trevor, with myself, Margaret

Aspinall and Sue Roberts. Trevor had been invited back because he had the skills needed to chair such an important executive committee. We were asked to go down to Westminster to meet with Michael Wills, the then Minister of State for Justice, who, along with PM Gordon Brown, are very much my unsung heroes in all of this. Michael and his team of lawyers worked very hard alongside the executive committee, and between us all we really started to get the process of retrieving the documents moving.

Work on the executive committee continued when the new Conservative government came into power in 2010, led by PM David Cameron and Home Secretary Theresa May. A cross-party consensus led to the setting up of the Hillsborough Independent Panel (HIP), which would be led by the Right Reverend James Jones and made up of nine members, from investigative journalists and researchers through to academics, each bringing their own area of expertise to ensure optimum disclosure of all the documents. In truth, after the miner's strike a few years before Hillsborough, I hadn't been surprised by Thatcher's response to the disaster, but I'd felt bitterly disappointed at the years the HFSG and the other families had spent fighting the Blair government to get at the truth, and now here we were finally being given access to the evidence under Cameron and May.

While working on the executive committee I was still employed at M&S. However, eventually I found that the committee work became all-consuming, requiring numerous trips to London for meetings with Theresa May, who in my opinion was the best Home Secretary we'd ever dealt with, and with the Ministry of Justice, or Kier Starmer who was the Director of Public Prosecutions (DPP) at the time. As much as I didn't want to, I decided to resign my position with M&S to concentrate on my work on the executive committee.

The HFSG had thirty-three family members at this time, and some families who'd formed their own group were also campaigning for the release of the documents. It took over three years of hard work by the HFSG executive committee, and the other families, before the HIP delivered their report in September 2012.

The contents of the documents we and the representatives of other families got to see were shocking but not surprising and bore out what we had suspected all along: lies, cover-ups, and dirty tricks. The HIP report, which was published in September 2012, was able to fully conclude that no Liverpool fans were in any way responsible for the disaster and that the main cause was a 'lack of police control'. Crowd safety had been 'compromised at every level'.

The hardest information for most of the families to hear was that as many as forty-one of the ninety-six who had died might have survived if the emergency services had properly responded to the disaster. This number is based on post-mortem examinations which found some victims may have had heart, lung or blood circulation function for some time after being removed from the crush. The report also stated that placing fans who were 'merely unconscious' on their backs, rather than in the recovery position, would have resulted in their deaths due to airway obstruction. That your child or, in my case, children could have survived if they had been attended to, while outside dozens of experienced medical staff stood by and did nothing, was a very bitter pill to swallow.

The report also disclosed, as we had suspected, that as many as 164 witness statements had been altered. This included 116 statements amended to remove or change negative comments about the South Yorkshire Police who, as requested by the coroner, performed blood–alcohol tests on the victims. The SYP had then run computer checks on the national police database on those with a non-zero alcohol level in an attempt to 'impugn the reputations of the deceased'. As well as the police passing on blatant lies about fans' culpability to the press, the report concluded that the Conservative MP for Sheffield Hallam, Irvine Patnick, had also fed the press lies. I wasn't surprised: for the Sheffield coroner and the police to try to malign the victims in this way was unforgivable and taking blood tests to do so, including from young schoolchildren, was lower than low.

On Wednesday, 12 September 2012, Professor Phil Scraton, the primary author of the Hillsborough Independent Panel's report, stood in Liverpool Anglican Cathedral in front of all the families and read out the conclusions of the HIP panel. There were 153 detailed findings, and Phil spoke for over an hour. As he finished, there was silence. Then together as one, the families – many in tears – stood to applaud.

Within minutes PM David Cameron, on a live link from the Houses of Parliament, addressed a packed House of Commons on the findings of the report. He said the findings in the report were 'deeply distressing', and that 'with the weight of the new evidence in the report it's right for me today as prime minister to make a proper apology to the families of the ninety-six . . . On behalf of the government, and indeed of our country, I am profoundly sorry that this double injustice has been left uncorrected for so long.'

It was not just an apology: it was a double apology. Not only for the events of that day, and the time it had taken to find the truth, but also for the cover-up that followed, and the government's part in that.

Cameron went on to say it would be for the attorney general, Dominic Grieve, to decide whether to apply to the high court to quash the original inquest and seek a new one, as the families were demanding. But he added that it was clear 'today's report raises vital questions which must be examined'.

Just over two weeks after the report came out, the Labour Party conference began in Manchester, and Margaret Aspinall and I were invited by ITV's *Granada Tonight* to speak to Jack Straw, who would also be present. We were being filmed in a small hotel bedroom, sitting across from him around a table, and I felt conscious of the camera and of being miked up. But as the conversation started to flow, I was made aware by one of the answers Straw gave that Lord Stuart-Smith had seen all of the evidence that the HIP had seen to draw their conclusions from – fourteen years earlier!

I was so shocked that I was no longer aware of the cameras and microphones, and, as he was speaking, I launched into, 'Just a minute Mr Straw! Are you really telling me that Stuart-Smith got to see all the documentation the HIP has just seen, only *fourteen years* earlier? And came to the conclusions that he did?'

Straw looked embarrassed and replied, 'Yes.'

I was astounded.

'Well,' I said, 'how sad is that, Mr Straw, that I have had to wait another fourteen years for the truth about my daughters' deaths.'

Margaret joined in, 'Do you think you might have appointed the wrong judge, Mr Straw?'

He answered, 'Yes.'

I thought Margaret had made such a good point. However, later I realised that to get the result Blair's government had wanted, he'd appointed *exactly* the right man. All of them in that cabinet knew what they'd seen in that documentation years earlier. They all knew what the truth was – and yet families had lost children, partners, parents and siblings, and they'd stitched us all up like this. There is no other word for it: corruption.

Prior to losing my daughters, I was naive about so many things and I would never ever have believed that this could go on in this country, from government and politicians through to the police. I had always respected those institutions. But I have seen it now first-hand, and I am no longer that same innocent person, and neither are those families and friends who have witnessed it with me, and that I think is a terrible shame. We should all expect the best of our institutions, but no, this was the Establishment covering up for its own.

Months later, in the days before Christmas 2012, the Lord Chief Justice, Igor Judge, and two other judges quashed the original verdict of accidental deaths. The families were there in the Royal Courts of Justice to hear it. This was the best Christmas present the families and I could have had, as it meant we'd get our new inquests. I went down to Allerton Cemetery and put flowers on the girls' grave.

There followed three years of hard work, and the executive committee became a full-time job for me and the others. It hasn't always been plain sailing, and the experience of working on the committee has taught me so much, especially how to work successfully alongside people who you might not necessarily get along with on a personal level. What is most important is that you all work together for the same goal, and achieve it.

We were asked to keep all our work on the Executive Committee confidential. This was difficult at times because I had very close ties with a number of group members. I respected this agreement and I knew that I could not break confidentiality. However, it was uncomfortable for me, because I fell out with a good friend over this and I don't believe that she ever forgave me. We had a special relationship following Hillsborough, and I found this hard to bear.

Personal integrity is very important to me, and I understood there had to be mutual trust on both sides. I did not want to do anything to jeopardise what we were trying to achieve. If I give my word on something, then I will not renege on this. Trust is one of my core values. This is why I have struggled with the police lies and cover-up since April 1989.

We had an extraordinary legal team, including the esteemed barrister Michael Mansfield QC, and Marcia Willis Stewart, the prominent human rights lawyer and honorary QC, and some of the most hardworking barristers and solicitors. They were completely unequalled in their dedication and commitment. By this stage, the member families in the HFSG had swelled to seventy-seven, as only families in the HFSG could be represented by this eminent team. Family members not in the HFSG were represented by their own groups of lawyers.

The second inquests began in Birchwood Park, Warrington, on 31 March 2014. It had taken a quarter of a century fighting for our loved ones to get to this point. Sadly, not all family members had made it; some had died, never recovering from their loss, and their children or even their children's children now represented their families. This time the inquests were held in Warrington so that it would be closer to Liverpool, whereas the first ones held in Sheffield had been difficult for the families to travel to every day. Jimmy McGovern accompanied me to the first day of the new inquests and sat alongside me in this vast room, crammed with lawyers, family members and the press. The atmosphere was tense. Then the jurors filed in and were asked to state if there was any reason why they couldn't sit on the jury. One of them went up to the judge and they had a murmured conversation for some minutes, then the judge turned to the room and told us, 'He says he's an Evertonian.' Despite all the heartache and struggles we had endured over the decades, the place erupted in laughter. Thank God for that Scouse sense of humour. It has certainly helped me many times.

On the day of the disaster, waiting to be identified, Vicki had been body number 89, and Sarah was body number 64. And since then, they have always been treated as just two of the ninety-six. At the second inquest, Sarah, Vicki and all the victims were treated as individuals. They were no longer identified by a number. They were real people who had lost real lives. It was wonderful the way that the second inquests were framed to allow us to give pen portraits of our loved ones and what they had meant to us. I was able to stand up and talk about my two beautiful daughters and what they did with their lives, and what they might have done in the future. It gave me my girls back, as I individualised my loss. It was so moving, sitting and listening every day to the other families' portraits of their lost loved ones; it made each person real. By the end of the inquest, I thought I'd got to know something about everyone who had died alongside my daughters that day.

Although I was proud of what the families of the ninety-six had achieved, and felt comfort in belonging to such a special group of people, there were drawbacks too. We were a democratic group, and there were times when my feelings as an individual, and the will of the majority of the group, didn't necessarily align. There was also guilt at individualising my own grief when others were suffering too.

During my counselling sessions a few years after the disaster, my counsellor had picked up on this: 'Jenni, you never talk about your own girls without saying, "along with ninety-four other people". You have got to learn you can't take on all the ninety-six deaths personally.'

The second inquest therefore allowed me to speak about Sarah and Vicki, but for the first time I did it without feeling guilty.

One of the witnesses who'd been dismissed by the coroner at the first inquest came and gave evidence at Birchwood

Park. I had always said that if Sarah could have got out of the crush but Vicki couldn't, then Sarah would have stayed there with her little sister. I was sure of that. At the second inquest we got the evidence. It came from another football supporter who said he was on the perimeter fence, outside pen 3 on the pitch side. He told the inquest he'd managed to climb up the fence and reach down and get hold of Sarah's hand. Both girls had been very distressed, but because Vicki was shorter, he couldn't reach her. But as he tried to pull Sarah up, she was saying, 'Please take care of my sister. My sister needs help.'

Sarah's biggest concern was not for herself but for her little sister. It was something I always knew. She would never, ever leave Vicki, even to save herself. Then the supporter said that Sarah's hand had slipped away from his.

The evidence was very moving, and it was the first time we'd heard it in twenty-six years. It had been there right from the first inquest, but it hadn't been allowed to be heard because it was after the 3.15 cut-off. Another witness, a policeman from the Norwich force, had been one of the Liverpool supporters who'd helped carry Sarah out on a hoarding. At the end of giving his evidence, he asked the coroner if he could speak directly to Mr and Mrs Hicks, please.

The coroner said, 'Only if you are very quick.'

The police officer then turned to us and said, 'I just wanted you to know that Sarah was not on her own. She had somebody with her who cared.'

Trevor and I went up to the officer afterwards and thanked him. We also thanked the kind supporter who had held

Sarah's hand and tried to get her out of the pen – it meant so very much to us. It was comforting to know there were people there who genuinely tried to help my daughters.

I had to accept many difficult things during those two years of the inquest. I would get up early and travel to Warrington, which is twenty miles away, every day. The only time I missed going for a few days was when I had to have surgery to remove a malignant tumour from my face. The surgeon was able to remove all the cancer and I got back to the inquest as soon as I could. As difficult as it was to hear the evidence being presented, finally we were getting the truth, and having waited this long I was not intending to miss any of it.

On the day the families were due to hear the verdict, the tension was palpable in the room. The moment for which we had now been waiting for twenty-six years was finally here. Jimmy had accompanied me on the train from Liverpool, and the other families on the train were anxious. But I had no doubt whatsoever that we were going to get the verdict we wanted: that the ninety-six were all unlawfully killed. After all's said and done, Duckenfield had admitted it under oath, to Paul Greaney QC, who represented the Police Federation.

We took our seats in the courtroom and waited. The jury of six women and three men had to answer fourteen questions relating to the events on the day of the disaster, 15 April 1989. Not just to prove that the victims had been unlawfully killed, but to exonerate the fans from any blame whatsoever.

One by one, the jury foreman answered those questions.

This had been two long years, one of the longest jury cases in British legal history.

Question six was, 'Are you satisfied, so that you are sure,

that those who died in the disaster were unlawfully killed?'

The jury's answer: 'Yes.'

The verdicts were unanimous: all ninety-six victims had been unlawfully killed. There was an enormous sense of relief in the room.

But we held our breath and waited for the verdict on the Liverpool fans.

Question seven, 'Was there any behaviour on the part of football supporters which caused or contributed to the dangerous situation at the Leppings Lane turnstiles?'

The jury's answer: 'No.'

There was a second part to this question: 'If your answer to the question above is "no", then was there any behaviour on the part of football supporters which may have caused or contributed to the dangerous situation at the Leppings Lane turnstiles?'

The jury's answer, again: 'No.'

A cheer went up. The court was packed, and there was an overspill annexe as well, and everybody cheered, applauded, hugged and burst into tears. Someone shouted, 'God bless the jury!' and the jurors were given a round of applause as they left.

Outside, the relatives gathered and spontaneously sang Liverpool Football Club's anthem 'You'll Never Walk Alone'. The supporters had rightly been exonerated, and there were tears of happiness and of sadness for those we had lost, and also of relief that we had finally got the verdict we should have had twenty-six years earlier.

Without the fans being acquitted, the unlawfully killed verdicts would have been unacceptable to me. The fans had saved lives that day, not caused deaths. There will always be a place for them in my heart, for what they had to deal with on that day.

We held a live TV press conference in a room adjacent to the court, and tea and coffee and sandwiches were served to the families, for those who could manage to eat them. The BBC invited me to accompany them back to Liverpool so I could record live TV and radio interviews for the early evening news. They drove Jimmy and me to St George's Hall, and I did the interviews on St George's plateau outside the hall. We were there until 8 p.m. that evening, when Jimmy and I took a taxi home. We dropped Jimmy off, and finally I was home. I was too tired to do anything but have a shower, get into my PJs and make myself a fish-finger sandwich.

Sometime after, I decided to rewatch Jimmy's programme *Hillsborough*. My friend, the wonderful, late Katy Jones had been the researcher and factual producer, and as I watched it, I was so proud of Katy. She'd got it all right. The cover-up, the cut-off point: she got every last detail of it right.

Jimmy's film was made almost twenty years before we got our second inquest. We knew the truth then – we just needed the documentation to prove it, and that is exactly what the Hillsborough Independent Panel did. And now the inquest had followed suit.

The cover-up is a national scandal, and families who were trying to deal with their grief had to contend with all the lies and corruption too, and fight for decades of their lives to get at the truth – some falling ill and dying in the process. But what we needed now was accountability for the victims. Because without accountability there could never be any justice.

Chapter 29

The day after the inquest an event was organised by Liverpool City Council at St George's Hall for the families and people of Liverpool, to acknowledge our hard-won verdict. When the families, the mayor and others emerged onto the steps of St George's Hall into the sunlight, all you could see was a mass of 30,000 people stretching all the way up Lime Street and back, all clapping and cheering. Among the crowd there was a huge banner with the words I will never forget: *They picked on the wrong city!*

Liverpool is unique in the way that the community comes together in times of adversity. When Trevor and I split up and I moved here from London, I could not have moved to a better place to be supported, and it's been a huge part of my journey and of finding myself again. So it was a good, good choice. I don't think any other city would have stood up and been counted like Liverpool did. I can't think of anywhere else where, after thirty years, there would still be the fight, the compassion and the love for the people who were lost that day, and for their families too.

Since leaving my job at M&S to work on the executive committee seven years previously, I had run into financial problems. The only capital I had was my home, which I'd paid cash for when I'd moved to Liverpool. I'd always envisaged having a roof over my head, come what may. I loved it there and it made me feel insecure to have to sell it. But I realised my only option was to sell my home and move into rented accommodation. I had no choice. I moved on a cold, snowy January day in 2016, right in the midst of the second inquest. Obviously not the best timing, but unavoidable.

When the removal men turned up, they were three Evertonians. But they couldn't have been more helpful, even though they knew I was a 'Red'. It only took them four hours to empty my house and move me to my rented flat ten minutes up the road. By the time they finished, the flat looked like I'd lived there for years. And next day one of the solicitors from the inquest, Sarah Flanagan, came to help me shift the last few boxes. They all helped make a very difficult move much easier for me.

Over the years Trevor had become very successful. He owned his own company, and he had worked long hours for all he had achieved. I was pleased that all the hard work and long hours had paid off – however, I was part of that for twenty-four years too: supporting him, working, and raising our family during what were prob-ably the hardest years when he was trying to make it in his ongoing career.

During the inquests at Warrington, I was surprised when Trevor came and sat next to me during a tea break, because he usually sat away from me. He told me he was thinking of retiring and sailing off in his yacht somewhere.

Why is he telling me this? I wondered.

He went on to tell me that he had decided to let me have some of what I believed to be a joint pension that related to the time of our marriage, which he said I was always going on about. He added, 'It won't be much.'

I didn't answer him. I just thought, *I'll believe that when it happens.*

In the end he didn't sell up and sail away. However, I decided it was perhaps time I got my affairs in order. I didn't have a will, an executor or any of the things I should have had. I didn't even have a next of kin. I made an appointment to see a solicitor, to sort out a will and anything else I might need. During the conversation with the solicitor, he asked about pensions. I told him about the pension Trevor had mentioned, which I was resigned to the fact I was never going to get.

My solicitor suggested I talked to a financial advisor, which I did. He went through all my finances, and again the subject of pensions came up. I told him about the conversation Trevor had had with me at the inquest, and his advice was to telephone Trevor and ask him if the offer was still open. So I called Trevor up, and his reaction was better than I thought it would be. He told me he'd look into it and get back to me.

I told him I was taking legal advice about the value of the pension. Trevor also instructed a lawyer and letters went back and forth between our two lawyers.

If my head had been in the right place, this should all have been sorted out at the time of our divorce. However, it was one of those life-defining moments when I saw the last offer from Trevor's lawyers. Trevor and I hadn't been close for a long time, but I'd felt there was always this invisible thread between us, an umbilical cord, linking me and Trevor to our two beautiful daughters.

I was offered £10,000, minus his legal fees. My pension contribution to twenty-four years of marriage to Trevor had been valued at £6,160.

I didn't take the money.

There have been many milestones on my journey. However, this was an important one for me. It was the reality check I needed, to finally put paid to the illusion that I would always have a small place in Trevor's heart, simply because I was Sarah and Vicki's mum. Just as Trevor had in mine, because he was the girls' dad. It was an important lesson I needed to learn. Finally, the umbilical cord was severed. It was difficult, but it became a positive thing for me, another very important step forward on my journey.

One of the most positive things that has happened to me since Hillsborough has been my involvement for the last ten years with the students and staff at the wonderful Harmonize Academy in Liverpool. It is an alternative provision, free school and is one of only five such schools across the country. The academy takes a broad range of children aged thirteen to eighteen. Some students are vulnerable and have been through a lot in their lives, and they come to Harmonize where there are small classes with a lot of support. You see them really begin to blossom and flourish under the guidance of Stephen Daley, Marie McConville, Carl Parkinson and Helena Mulhearn. But the academy is not an end to it – it is just the start. When the students finish here, they go on to further education, appropriate work experience, job opportunities and training. It is truly an outstanding school, and I am so proud to be on the board of governors and to be invited to give talks to the students here at times. They inspire me to do better.

The school has the ethos of trust, respect, compassion and forgiveness. After the venality of Hillsborough, what better mantra for life could there be? At the school we employ our own psychologists, and the young people here truly learn to succeed. I wish we could have schools like this all over the country and can't praise the students and staff highly enough.

I first became involved through Dr Tani Omideyi, Pastor and Chair of Liverpool Lighthouse, and a founder member of the academy, when he ran the Love & Joy Gospel Choir who sang at each anniversary of Hillsborough, held at Anfield. In 2011, Pastor Tani came up to me and said, 'After the service I'd like to chat about something that I think would be perfect for you.'

I wonder if he wants me to join the choir? I thought, which with my voice I wasn't sure would be a good idea. But when I spoke to him later that day, he surprised me when he said, 'I would like you to be a governor of the new academy school I am setting up.'

I was both flattered and nervous, and I remember going to the first meeting. Everybody sat round the table introduced themselves, all of them highly qualified teachers and professionals. When it got to me at the end, I said, 'Hi, I'm Jenni Hicks and I don't know what I'm doing here.'

Everyone burst into laughter, but it was true because I felt I was so unqualified. Though as it turned out, everyone was in a conventional sense, but we each had a special kind of skill to bring to the project.

So I became one of the founder members of Harmonize, which means I am a member of the governing body – shaping its policies and the direction it goes in. My friend Jimmy McGovern was invited to officially open the school, along with the High Sheriff of Merseyside. The drama department put on a musical based on Jimmy's *Hillsborough* docudrama. We were all sitting in the performance hall, not sure what to expect, when the students came on and performed an excerpt. The young girl playing my part was very pretty and very fit, and could do cartwheels and backflips, and I said to Jimmy, 'Just like me!'

At other times I have brought in Andy Burnham, a former Liverpool MP who is now Metro Mayor of Greater Manchester, and Steve Rotherham, Metro Mayor of the Liverpool City Region, to talk to the young people and to see what we do here. I haven't been able to be as good a governor as I would have liked, as I spent most of 2019 at the manslaughter trial of David Duckenfield at Preston Crown Court, for which the school kindly gave me a sabbatical. But I have made it to the Everyman Theatre to see the young people's performances there, and I have led workshops with the students and spoken about my experiences at Hillsborough.

I feel my work at Harmonize is the thing that Sarah and Vicki would be most proud of me for, and I know they would love it there too. While I may have helped some of the students here, working with them has certainly helped me with my Hillsborough issues. It's not just about the grief of losing your children, and in my case, your marriage and your home too, but there's the other side of all that went on – the cover-up and the dirty tricks campaign. So, it's good to have something decent and good like this, and I feel so blessed and privileged to be involved with Harmonize Academy.

Chapter 30

After the second inquest, the CPS took the evidence they needed from it to charge David Duckenfield with gross negligence manslaughter. I was pleased about this, although I later wondered why he hadn't also been charged with perverting the course of justice like the others. It was not until January 2019 that the trial began at Preston Crown Court, with a link to the Cunard Building in Liverpool for families who didn't wish to travel to Preston.

Once again, the charges brought against Duckenfield only related to ninety-five victims, because eighteen-year-old Tony Bland had died later than a year and a day after his injuries. But it is about Tony too: how could you ever leave Tony out, for God's sake? The poor lad was in a persistent vegetative state from that first day until his family were finally permitted to switch off his life-support almost four years later, so Tony will always be included by all the families. We may be ninety-five in court, but we are ninety-six in spirit and the same goes for outside of the courtroom; we are all in agreement on that.

This was a CPS prosecution, which meant, for the first time in thirty years, the families had no legal representation whatsoever. We were told that we wouldn't be given the opportunity to discuss the case with the QCs and legal teams involved. However, representatives of six families who attended court every day in Preston had different ideas. These were Lou Brookes, who had lost her brother; Chrissie Burke and her two brothers Stephen and Ian and her daughter Shereen, who had lost their dad and granddad; Christine McEvoy, who had lost her daughter; Jackie Gilhooley, whose ten-year-old son Jon-Paul had died in the disaster; and me, representing Sarah and Vicki. We would be joined by other families when their work permitted, including Debbie Matthews and her daughter Deanna, and Evelyn Mills, and we all remained the core people attending both the trial and retrial. We should all feel proud of the challenges we made and what we achieved, and how there wasn't anything more we could have done for our loved ones.

We held regular meetings with the CPS prosecution QCs and made challenge after challenge throughout the prosecution. Without the challenges we made, evidence that should have been heard in court would not have been heard. This included David Duckenfield's admission at the second inquest, under oath, of causing the ninety-six deaths.

We also challenged the decision to allow Duckenfield to sit in the well of the court alongside his legal team, when he should have been in the dock like any other defendant in a criminal case. He sat there all day, in his expensive suit, playing on his computer. It made it very difficult for the jury to distinguish between him and his lawyers! It wasn't rocket science to see that this could put him at an advantage in the minds of the jury, and in my opinion was the most shameful bias. Duckenfield also refused to give evidence at the trial, just as he had back at the private prosecution in 2000. He has never stood in a criminal court and given evidence, and been cross-examined by the prosecution.

As the case wore on, we began to think that the two QCs the CPS had chosen to prosecute weren't fit for purpose – or perhaps they had been chosen for that very reason. The trial ended with the jury not being able to reach a verdict. A retrial was ordered and set down for that October. I didn't welcome this, if I'm honest. I would have settled for a hung jury verdict the first time around, because my biggest fear was that Duckenfield would be found not guilty.

In the weeks after the first trial I wrote to Sue Hemming, Director of Legal Services at the CPS, with copies to the DPP and the Attorney General, saying that I disagreed with the retrial, but if there had to be a retrial then it needed to be with a different judge. Because in his summing up to the jury, I and others felt that Judge Openshaw had nailed his colours to the mast. By drawing attention to certain evidence, and telling the jury to disregard other evidence, there was no doubt in my mind, or that of the other families there, that he showed bias. He had taken us back to the original inquests in 1990–91, which three High Court judges had found to be unreliable.

The retrial began in October 2019 in Preston, and the same six families took their seats in the court, and again there was a link to the Cunard Building. And disgracefully, despite the families' protests, the same judge was presiding. Duckenfield again refused to give evidence, and when he was taken to hospital with a chest infection during the trial, the judge referred to him as 'poor chap' to the jury. Lou Brooks, Chris Burke and I just looked at each other in horror and disbelief. I'm sure it must have been the same in the Cunard Building in Liverpool where some of the families were watching by live link-up.

And it got worse: the judge spoke at great length about Duckenfield's PTSD, describing all the symptoms, and his lack of empathy, and telling the jurors not to draw an 'adverse inference against him' for showing no emotion. With all that the families had suffered, did our own trauma and loss – including the suicides, broken marriages and deaths caused by broken hearts along the way – not equate to what this 'poor chap' had suffered? And that is before you even consider what the victims who'd died that day had suffered. You only had to look at the photographs on the green baize board outside the gymnasium that day to understand that. Or look at your loved ones in body bags. Given that Judge Openshaw was able to correspond so favourably on Duckenfield's behalf to the jury, it was obvious what was going on here. Duckenfield was going to be found not guilty, even though he'd admitted under oath, while being cross-examined by Paul Greaney QC at the second inquest, that he was guilty of causing all ninety-six deaths, that he'd ordered gate C to be opened, and that he had lied about it afterwards and blamed the fans.

At the second inquest the coroner repeatedly told the jury that to bring in a verdict of unlawful killing they had to be sure it was a case of 'gross negligence manslaughter to a criminal standard'. But as Tony Evans of the *Independent* newspaper wrote:

> . . . the judge's direction made the acquittal almost inevitable.
>
> The judge said the inquests were 'quite irrelevant' because 'the rules and procedures were very different to a criminal

trial'. Effectively, the jury were told that the longest inquest in British history was to be treated as meaningless when it came to deciding whether or not David Duckenfield's conduct had been criminal. Benjamin Myers QC, Duckenfield's barrister, repeatedly alleged that Liverpool fans arrived late at the stadium, that ticketless fans had an impact on the disaster, that alcohol was a factor and that supporters refused to follow the directions of the police.

All of these suggestions had been refuted by the inquest.

This verdict does not override or undo the inquest's results. It is almost incomprehensible to imagine that no one will be held responsible for the deaths of 96 people – one of the victims died later so Duckenfield was charged over the 95 that were killed on the day. The actions of the chief superintendent who made the fatal decision to open the outside gates and allow 2,000 ticket-bearing fans to come into the ground in an unregulated surge were found not to be criminal.

In my opinion, the judge's summing up was outrageously sympathetic to Duckenfield. Mr Justice Openshaw even suggested – despite the matchday commander admitting at the inquest that he told Graham Kelly, the FA's chief executive, that fans had forced the gates – that Duckenfield may not have lied. The judge said that the defendant might have genuinely believed that the gates had been broken down. To me, the logic did not make the slightest bit of sense.*

* *Independent*, 28 November 2019; https://www.independent.co.uk/sport/football/premier-league/hillsborough-disaster-manslaughter-verdict-david-duckenfield-justice-tony-evans-a9225186.html. Reprinted with permission. © Tony Evans/*Indpendent*

★

Tony Evans' account was spot on in my opinion: the judge's summing up took us right back to the first inquest. But the evidence from the first inquest had been deemed unreliable, and the verdict quashed. Three high court judges had found this evidence unreliable. It beggared belief, and it made no sense. Once again it was the Establishment propping itself up, and I wondered what my girls would have made of it all. When I was interviewed outside court after the not guilty verdict, I stressed that in my opinion an ordinary Crown Court is an inadequate venue to deal with a case of this magnitude thirty-one years after the event.

So, we've got to live with the fact that all of our loved ones were unlawfully killed – but without anyone being held accountable for the deaths.

Writing this book now, it is clear to me that the Duckenfield trials in Preston were a premeditated farce. Yet another trip down the rabbit hole to the Mad Hatter's tea party. The QCs appointed by the CPS were not fit for purpose and totally out of their depth. It was obvious the judge had already decided David Duckenfield was not guilty. A whole year of taxpayers' money totally wasted. A whole year of families' wounds being ripped open yet again. A whole year of South Yorkshire Police and the State rewriting history. Families were made to sit in a dungeon of a courtroom in the basement of Preston Crown Court, a public gallery enclosed by glass on either side, facing the press, not the court, to prevent us from looking at the jury. The families weren't legally represented, and in the retrial the defence lawyers suggested that we should not only be kept behind glass, but the glass should be covered so the jury wouldn't have sight of the families.

The answer has to be that there's something behind all of this: something that those in power have decided it's not in the public interest to know.

We are now at the end of the line, as we have been told there's nowhere else left for us to go as far as David Duckenfield is concerned. Unsurprisingly, many of the families were in tears. When you have fought so hard for so long and you realise there is never going to be anyone held accountable for their actions that day, it is very hard to deal with. In fact, there has only ever been one person found guilty of any wrongdoing in the Hillsborough disaster, and that is Graham Mackrell from Sheffield Wednesday football club. He was tried along-side Duckenfield in the first trial at Preston Crown Court too, and fined £6,500 plus £5,000 costs, which – when you consider he was the safety officer at the club that day – seems to me to be no more than a slap on the wrist.

During my journey, I have seen the worst of people, and I've seen the best of people. After the desperately disappointing verdict at Duckenfield's retrial, it was the best of people I chose to see. And on the day of the verdict, local boy and Liverpool player Trent Alexander-Arnold and club captain Jordan Henderson laid ninety-six beautiful red roses at the Hillsborough Memorial outside Anfield on behalf of the team. The roses were accompanied by a heartfelt note: 'In memory of the ninety-six and solidarity with the families and survivors. With love, the Liverpool players.'

Liverpool legend Kenny Dalglish also posted a message of support on Twitter:

> Like anyone who has seen at close quarters the dignified way that the families have conducted themselves in their fight for justice, Marina and I are hugely disappointed by Thursday's verdict.
>
> We had hoped that the families would get the outcome that they wanted and that they clearly deserved, but that hasn't proven to be the case. The rest of us must now continue to offer whatever support they might need.
>
> From a personal point of view, I am immensely proud of everything that the families and their supporters have achieved over the last three decades. In the face of tragedy and with so much against them, they have persevered with the utmost integrity and in a way that shames all who have let them down.
>
> I know there cannot be any consolation in a situation like this but I would hope that they can take some comfort from the fact that so many good people will still stand beside them.

There has been so much support, but I can't help thinking that if David Duckenfield had had the courage to hold his hands up over three decades ago, and take ownership of his actions on 15 April 1989 that led to the deaths of the ninety-six, and not put the families through years and years of having to seek truth and accountability for our loved ones, then perhaps over time I could have found some kind of forgiveness for him. After all, we are all human beings and make mistakes. But for him to continue to blame the innocent victims and fans for his own incompetence is unforgivable. He didn't just let down the people who died, he let down his colleagues too – and he's still letting down all the many police officers who take pride in their jobs and wear their uniforms with honour.

On Monday, 19 April 2021, at the Lowry Theatre on Salford Quays, the final trial connected to the Hillsborough disaster began. Two former police officers and a solicitor were accused of perverting the course of justice, in what was widely known as 'the cover-up trial'. The accused were: Peter Metcalf, seventy-two, a former solicitor for the South Yorkshire Police and partner at law firm Hammond Suddards; the then Chief Superintendent Donald Denton, eighty-three; and Detective Chief Inspector Alan Foster, seventy-four. They had been accused of changing sixty-eight officers' statements to mask the failings of the force.

On Wednesday, 26 May, less than halfway through the time allotted for the trial, the judge, Mr Justice William Davis, ruled there was no legal case to answer as the amended statements were prepared for Lord Justice Taylor's public inquiry into the tragic events. Davis said the Taylor Inquiry was not a statutory public inquiry, where evidence was given on oath, but an 'administrative exercise', so it was not a 'course of public justice' that could be perverted.

I attended the trial every day, taking the train from Liverpool to Manchester Deansgate, then the tram to Media City. I would leave home at 8 a.m. and return home at 6.30 p.m., which left little time but to shower, eat and prepare for the next day. I've sat in numerous courtrooms, but to sit in a theatre seemed to take away the seriousness of what was being addressed by the court.

The public gallery was on the balcony, and we were looking down at the circle where all the media were sitting. Where the seating for the stalls would have been there were rows of barristers and solicitors, the front row for the prosecution and three rows of defence behind them. Opposite, on the other side of the stalls, was the jury, facing the legal teams. And there on the stage was the Judge, dressed all in red and white, looking like Father Christmas. Being in a theatre, with its red seats and theatre lighting, and no windows, it was hard not to feel we were there to witness a performance. And I guess it was a kind of performance, because that's what QCs and barristers do.

Much to my displeasure, most of the evidence had been agreed in advance, so there were very few witnesses called. Various witness statements were read out by a member of the Independent Office for Police Conduct (IOPC), and as far as I'm concerned, the whole thing was a farce. I kept likening it to an episode of Monty Python, expecting Michael Palin and John Cleese to pop up at any given moment. I even thought the court usher came from the Ministry of Silly Walks. At the end of the first week, a jury member asked a question to the judge: 'What are we supposed to be deciding here?' So they were as confused as we were.

One of the most difficult parts of the trial was when the judge announced there was no case to answer, he instructed the Foreman of the Jury to read out verdicts of 'not guilty' on each of the five counts, for each of the three accused, even though they hadn't really been tried. Hearing those words fifteen times seemed needlessly cruel on the families listening above.

Jonathan Goldberg QC, counsel for Peter Metcalf, has since been criticised for saying on Radio 5 Live that the behaviour of the Liverpool fans was 'perfectly appalling' and effectively the cause of the tragedy. He said his words had been 'taken out of context and badly misunderstood'. Whatever he intended to say, he came across as repeating the outrageous, damning and untrue accusations regarding the Liverpool fans, who had previously been exonerated of any blame. Complaints have been made, and his comments have been condemned in every quarter.

Nine days later, the following Friday, on 4 June 2021, South Yorkshire and West Midlands Police admitted a campaign to avoid responsibility for the Hillsborough disaster, and blaming the fans and victims instead, which myself and the bereaved families call a cover-up.

Both forces have agreed a settlement to pay compensation to families whose relatives were among the ninety-six men, women and children who were unlawfully killed at Hillsborough that day, and to the survivors, for additional trauma and psychiatric damage caused by the police's actions.

The financial recompense is for the psychiatric injuries the families and survivors have suffered and to pay for treatment or counselling. The civil claims, alleging misfeasance in a public office, were first made in September 2015 during the new inquests into how the ninety-six people died.

So this means there's never going to be any accountability in a criminal court for those ninety-six innocent victims of the Hillsborough disaster. The campaign was never about money, it was about accountability. The police have now admitted all they were accused of. However, in the last of the criminal trials, the court found there's no case to answer. How can that be just? Something has to change.

In his introductory remarks in the final court case, Davis proudly stated that nothing much had changed in the criminal courts since the Middle Ages. I was astounded by these remarks. The law should never be static. It should always be a work in progress.

I now believe that the criminal justice system isn't set up to deal with a case of this magnitude, taking place three decades after the event. There needs to be a different system. Lord Michael Wills' and Maria Eagle MP's Public Advocate Bill needs to be made law without delay, as this will protect anyone else from being treated the way the families of the ninety-six unlawfully killed victims at Hillsborough were treated. There also needs to be a duty of candour from those in authority and public service to tell the truth, and not hide behind their positions or uniforms. What better legacy for the ninety-six and all those affected by the Hillsborough disaster?

The cover-up has prevented healing. All the lies, corruption and lack of accountability keeps reopening wounds that are desperately trying to heal. It has prevented us from dealing with our grief properly.

I think the biggest insult of all is the way the Establishment continues to cover up for itself, patronise and underestimate the intelligence of the families, survivors and everybody affected by the Hillsborough disaster.

One year on from the publication of this book, the response from all 47 police forces in England and Wales to the 2017 Bishop James Jones report (the 'Patronizing Disposition of Unaccountable Power') was released on 31st January 2023. The response included the police apology over the failings over Hillsborough, stating 'the profound failings of policing that led to the Hillsborough disaster and for the pain and suffering endured for years by the families of those unlawfully killed'. They have also pledged a new code of ethics and cultural change.

The recommendations made by Bishop James Jones in his report have been adopted by the Hillsborough Law Now campaign. I await the the government's response to the report and the IOPC report, expected shortly and which has so far taken ten years to write. My hope is that the Hillsborough Law Now will become a priority and be enacted into law. There has to be a duty of candor for all those in public office. We have to have an independent public advocate, and we have to have a level playing field of funding. Those with power should never be unaccountable.

Epilogue

Who knows what was lost that day? On the day my children died. Not just my children: my children's children, their children's children, and on it goes. Their input into the world, all lost.

I do sometimes allow myself to chase rainbows and imagine what Sarah and Vicki's partners would have been like, what my grandchildren would have been like, what it would have been like to have a family that has grown instead of diminished. What my life would have been like if we hadn't gone to that football match on 15 April 1989. Over the years, I have watched how my closest friends' lives have moved on. For me it has been thirty years of not quite fitting in – I'm a fully paid-up member of the awkward squad when it comes to things like that. No matter how kind people try to be, I will always be on the periphery of that kind of life. I can't chase rainbows any more.

I am sometimes referred to as a victim: I am not the victim here – my daughters are. They are the ones who lost their lives that day. If I have been the victim of anything, it's the cover-up. Back in the 1980s, when Maggie Thatcher was in power, Sarah, Vicki, Trevor and I could have been a Thatcherite poster family – in many ways we were. I wonder perhaps if this is why the media picked up on us.

And yet it was Thatcher's government who I believe put in place the cover-up that we've been fighting all this time. Those stolen years, when I should have been healing, but was not able to.

In my childhood home, there was an ethos of right's right and wrong's wrong, and not a lot of room for many shades of grey. And if you saw wrongdoing, you spoke up. I guess that's embodied in me, although through life experience I now recognise there are many shades of grey.

How could something so simple become so complicated? How could so many people dedicate so much time and effort to keeping a lie alive? I am still waiting for South Yorkshire Police to do the honourable thing. For David Duckenfield to speak up and tell the whole truth. Because of them, I have lost an extra three decades of my life. However, I've worked hard at not becoming bitter because I realise how damaging that can be. All the numerous enquiries, investigations, scrutinies and court cases have prevented the grieving process from taking its course, thus not giving my open wounds an opportunity to heal.

I've never wanted pity, or people feeling sorry for me. Compassion is OK; we all need compassion for what we've gone through. Instead, I know how lucky I am ever to have been Sarah and Vicki's mum. The two greatest gifts I have ever had.

People say I am brave, but I question it. Risking your own life to rescue someone, that is bravery. I am not brave. I didn't choose to have to deal with this. It was something thrust upon me. I have had to live alongside an injustice so huge that nobody should ever have to bear. The grief and the loss never go away, you simply have to try and learn how to live with them.

I have always tried to make the best of the good things I have in life, and when I look back now, I realise just how far I've come. I have learned the painful process of living with the loss and the injustice, both running alongside each other. Which is a great achievement for me, as I never thought I would survive a second without Sarah and Vicki. I've had the kind of support you expect, the kind of support you ask for and the kind of support that shows up at the right time. I call these latter people my 'earth angels'.

My life isn't what I expected, but I've tried very hard to make it as good as it can be under the circumstances. Sometimes I succeed, sometimes not. I liken it to a roller-coaster ride, with all of its ups and downs. I was lost for a long time, and I am still learning to cope with the enormity of my daughters' deaths, and its consequences. Every day is different, but I've got to keep walking forward. I have begun to find myself again; however, in some ways it is a new me. I'm not the same person I was before. This whole experience has made me a stronger, more resilient and kinder person. I have also finally accepted that I am now and will always be a chipped cup and that only with self-love and self-care can I help prevent that chipped cup from breaking.

People are curious why I haven't found a new love in my life, but my friend Mark got it right when he said that's because I'm 'searching for a unicorn'. I think I've stopped looking for my unicorn, but who knows when a unicorn might turn up? I haven't given up hope. I haven't given up hope of anything. Maybe someday celebrity chef and broadcaster Simon Rimmer will come and whisk me away . . .

I've learned how positive it has been to admit the mental health issues, the depression, anxiety, fears and panic attacks I've had to face. Recently, celebrities and sportspeople have talked openly about their mental health issues. Even Prince William and Prince Harry. People are not hiding these things any more. And that has helped me not to feel guilty, to be open and honest about the issues I have to deal with. As more people talk openly about it, it has helped me to be open about it too. I thank them all for that.

I am also proud that Sarah, Vicki and I have been given the Freedom of the City of Liverpool, along with the other families. We had Mayors Steve Rotheram and Joe Anderson to thank for that honour. You only have to mention Hillsborough in Liverpool to see the outpouring of kindness and support you get from its people. It is special. I could not live in a better city and wish I had moved here years ago, so that Sarah and Vicki could've been brought up with this great sense of community, which has kindness and caring at the heart of it. It reminds me of the ethos and values of Longfield School that the girls went to in Pinner all those years ago. I do believe I have found my true home here and another kind of family among these special people. No wonder Sarah had wanted to stay after her degree course finished. And now of course she and Vicki are here to stay.

On the days when I feel particularly down, I blame myself for introducing my daughters to football and LFC.

But then I remember the good times we all had going to games as a family.

As for LFC, since Hillsborough the club has tried to do their best to support the victims' families. It must be very difficult for them to try and please ninety-six families, all with their individual needs and expectations. However, they continue to support and do their best to carry out the families' wishes, especially the current chairman Tom Werner, CEO Billy Hogan, and directors of communications Susan Black and Craig Evans. The disaster is woven into the fabric of the club, just as the '96' logo is there on every shirt of every player, and will always be. It is so important to the club and the fans that those victims will never be forgotten. And that is a comfort to me.

The club facilitates the memorial service every year, and the teams and officials from the club always attend. I have had the pleasure of meeting many of my heroes from the past: greats including Kenny (Dalglish), Rushy (Ian Rush), Aldo (John Aldridge), Macca (Steve McMahon), Barnesy (John Barnes) and Brucie (Bruce Grobbelaar). The team Sarah and Vicki knew and loved. They will always be 'my boys', 'the special ones'. And now Mr Klopp has given me my joy back in football with his fantastic team of players – Salah, Henderson, Mane, Van Dijk, Firmino – to name but a few. They have reminded me why Trevor, Sarah and Vicki and I travelled from London to Liverpool for every Saturday home game, to watch Liverpool FC play. Although I've never had the pleasure of meeting him, I have adopted Roberto Firmino into the family I have created of Steve, Mark, Rachel and, new addition, my 'nephew' Bobby Firmino.

★

It's the little everyday things I miss the most: the hugs, and the I love yous.

However, I try to focus on what Sarah said to me in the weeks before she and Vicki died: 'I want you to always remember that you couldn't have given me a better life, Mum. I could not have picked a better life for myself.'

I will forever be thankful for the honour of being Sarah and Vicki's mum, and lucky to have had them for the short time I had. I'm grateful for every second of the time I was privileged to spend with them.

My girls will always walk alongside me. I am not walking alone.

Acknowledgements

David Peat, my baby brother, now sadly deceased. I owe so much of my survival to you, David. Thank you, with love.

Our friends, neighbours, and families of my daughters' friends in Hatch End and the surrounding areas.

The numerous people worldwide who sent cards, letters and flowers to Trevor and me after the girls died.

Ann Adlington
John and Joan Aldridge
Mayor Joe Anderson
Susan Black
My three Evertonian movers from Britannia Removals Company
Gordon Brown
Bill Bygroves
Chris Burke and family
Andy Burnham
Sir Bobby and Lady Norma Charlton
Chris Conway
Kenny and Marina Dalgleish
Stephen Daley
Yadira Da Trindade
David Dein

Doctor Donnelly
Alan Dunkley
Mark Dunwell and family
Craig Evans
Sarah Flanagan
Jill Fudge
George and Mamie
Jackie Gilhooly
Ralph, Marie Hadley and family
Steven Hamill of Essential Hair and Beauty, who always tries
to make me look my best for the cameras
Phil and Hilda Hammond
The staff at Huyton station, Liverpool
Billy Hogan, CEO of LFC
Sue Johnston
Doreen Jones and family
Bishop James Jones
Katy Jones
Doctor King
Chris and Jeff Knightbridge
Matt Kylie
Katie Langridge
Julie Lau
Rachel Lester
Valerie Mandelson
Mike Mansfield
Jeanette McCabe
Graham McCombie
Marie McConville
Barbara McCoy

Evelyn McDonald

Charles McDougal

Colin McKeown of LA Productions

Jimmy McGovern (my bag-carrier) and Eileen McGovern

Amy McGuinness

Lucinda McNeile

Ru Merritt

Maddie Mogford

Doctor Morton

Helene Mulhearn

Paul Murphy

My colleagues at M&S Gemini, Warrington

Norma and Mike

Dr Tani Omideyi

Graham Owen

Landlord of the pub at The Queens Arms, next to Huyton Station

Carl Parkinson

Delores Peat

The postman in Hatch End

Sean Richardson

Rose and Bernie Robinson

Tracy, Paul, Peter and Claire Robinson, Tracy's partner Joe, and Paul's wife Sue

Sarah Robson

Metro Mayor Steve Rotheram

Sharon Ruddock of LA Productions

Nicola Shindler

The staff at South Parkway railway station, Liverpool

Paul Stark

Carol Thomas
Ellen Turner
Anna Valentine
The staff of Village Taxis at Garston, Liverpool
Matt, Kylie and Issy Walker
Tom Werner, Chairman of LFC
Marcia Willis-Stewart
Lord Michael Wills, my unsung hero
Ed Wilson, who's kept my head above water on several occasions
Steve Zahab and family

If there's anyone else I've forgotten, please forgive me.

All the fans and the people of Liverpool who've supported our campaign since 1989 and have walked alongside me on this journey.

About the Author

Jenni Hicks was the vice chair, and the longest-serving committee member, of the Hillsborough Families Support Group. She fought for justice for her daughters, and the other ninety-four victims of the Hillsborough disaster, for over three decades, and continues to campaign for Maria Eagle MP's and Lord Michael Wills' Public Advocate Bill, and and the Public Authority (Acccountability) Bill that calls for transparency, candour and frankness from the Police and public authorities.

Her story was featured in Jimmy McGovern's 1996 film, *Hillsborough*, starring Christopher Eccleston and Annabelle Apsion, but she has not spoken personally about her private life and journey as a mother until now. Jenni lives in Liverpool, and volunteers as a school governor for young people who have been excluded from mainstream education.

Author's Note

Since writing of the book was completed, the HFSG ceased to exist as of 1 January 2021.

On 27 July 2021, thirty-two years after suffering horrendous injuries in the Hillsborough disaster, Andrew Devine sadly passed away. A coroner's inquest in Liverpool on 28 July 2021 ruled he was unlawfully killed as a result of the disaster, making him the ninety-seventh victim. Andrew's name will now be added to the memorial at Anfield, and all the players' shirts and club logos will now reflect that there are ninety-seven victims of Hillsborough, not ninety-six. May you rest in peace, Andrew.

Victims of the Hillsborough Disaster

Jack Anderson	62 years
Colin Mark Ashcroft	19 years
James Gary Aspinall	18 years
Kester Roger Marcus Ball	16 years
Gerard Baron (Snr)	67 years
Simon Bell	17 years
Barry Bennett	26 years
David John Benson	22 years
David William Birtle	22 years
Paul David Brady	20 years
Andrew Mark Brookes	26 years
Carl Brown	18 years
Steven Brown	25 years
Henry Thomas Burke	47 years
Peter Andrew Burkett	24 years
Paul William Carlile	19 years
Raymond Thomas Chapman	50 years
Gary Christopher Church	19 years
Joseph Clark 'Oey'	29 years
Paul Clark	18 years
Gary Collins	22 years

Stephen Paul Copoc	20 years
Tracey Elizabeth Cox	23 years
James Philip Delaney	19 years
Christopher Barry Devonside	18 years
Chris Edwards	29 years
Vincent Michael Fitzsimmons	34 years
Steve Fox	21 years
Jon-Paul Gilhooley	10 years
Barry Glover	27 years
Ian Thomas Glover	20 years
Derrick George Godwin	24 years
Roy Hamilton	34 years
Philip Hammond	14 years
Eric Hankin	33 years
Peter Andrew Harrison	15 years
Gary Harrison	27 years
Stephen Francis Harrison	31 years
Dave Hawley	39 years
James Robert 'Jimmy' Hennessy	29 years
Paul Anthony Hewitson	26 years
Carl Hewitt	17 years
Nick Hewitt	16 years
Sarah Louise Hicks	19 years
Victoria Jane Hicks	15 years
Gordon Horn 'Goffer'	20 years
Arthur Horrocks	41 years
Thomas Howard	39 years
Tommy Anthony Howard	14 years
Eric George Hughes	42 years
Alan Johnston	29 years

Christine Anne Jones	27 years
Gary Philip Jones	18 years
Richard Jones B.Sc.	25 years
Nicholas Peter Joynes	27 years
Anthony P. Kelly	29 years
Michael Kelly	38 years
Carl David Lewis	18 years
David William Mather	19 years
Brian Christopher Matthews	38 years
Francis Joseph McAllister	27 years
John McBrien	18 years
Marian Hazel McCabe	21 years
Joe McCarthy	21 years
Peter McDonnell	21 years
Alan McGlone 'Gloney'	28 years
Keith McGrath	17 years
Paul Brian Murray	14 years
Lee Nicol	14 years
Stephen Francis O'Neill	17 years
Jonathon Owens	18 years
William Roy Pemberton	23 years
Carl Rimmer	21 years
Dave Rimmer	38 years
Graham John Roberts (HND)	24 years
Steven Robinson	17 years
Henry Charles Rogers	17 years
Andrew Sefton	23 years
Inger Shah	38 years
Paula Ann Smith	26 years
Adam Edward Spearritt	14 years

Philip John Steele   15 years
David Leonard Thomas   23 years
Pat Thompson   35 years
Peter Reuben Thompson   30 years
Stuart Thompson   17 years
Peter F. Tootle   21 years
Christopher James Traynor   26 years
Martin Kevin Traynor   16 years
Kevin Tyrrell   15 years
Colin Wafer   19 years
Ian 'Ronnie' Whelan   19 years
Mr. Martin Kenneth Wild   29 years
Kevin Daniel Williams   15 years
Graham John Wright   17 years
Tony Bland   22 years
Andrew Stanley Devine   55 years

Credits